Brothers Christian

First Lessons in English Grammar

used by the Brothers of the Christian schools

Brothers Christian

First Lessons in English Grammar
used by the Brothers of the Christian schools

ISBN/EAN: 9783337300135

Printed in Europe, USA, Canada, Australia, Japan

Cover: Foto ©Paul-Georg Meister /pixelio.de

More available books at **www.hansebooks.com**

FIRST LESSONS

IN

ENGLISH GRAMMAR

USED BY THE

BROTHERS OF THE CHRISTIAN SCHOOLS

NEW YORK
WM. H. SADLIER, Publisher
11 Barclay Street

Copyright, 1890
By JOHN P. MURPHY.

PREFACE.

THE present text-book is prepared as an introduction to the *Principles of English Grammar* on which it is based.

It purports to give only the bare essentials of the subject, illustrating definitions and rules with copious examples suited to the intelligence of beginners. It is to be hoped that teachers will find it an easy stepping-stone by which the young pupil will be enabled to ascend to a more thorough knowledge of our language.

NEW YORK, *September*, 1890.

Introductory Lessons
in
ENGLISH GRAMMAR.

INTRODUCTION.

1. The ordinary mode of communicating our thoughts is that of words.

2. Words are vocal sounds expressing a distinct meaning.

3. Vocal sounds are sounds of the human voice produced by certain organs of speech.

> The organs of speech are the tongue, the throat, the palate, the teeth, the lips, and the nose.

4. Written words are formed of letters.

5. Letters are certain signs invented to represent certain vocal sounds.

6. Letters are either vowels or consonants.

7. A vowel is a letter representing an open sound.

> There are five vowels; namely, a, e, i, o, u. All the other letters of the alphabet are consonants.

8. A consonant is a letter representing a sound formed by direct contact of the organs of speech; as, m, d, p.

9. Language is the expression of thought by means of words.

10. Language may be either spoken or written.

11. Spoken language is the expression of thought by means of the voice.

12. **Written language** is the expression of thought by means of written or printed characters.

13. **Grammar** is the science of the elementary forms of language. These elementary forms are words, phrases, and idioms.

I.

THE SENTENCE.

1. A **sentence** is a combination of words expressing a thought or judgment.
2. Every sentence contains a **subject** and a **predicate**.
3. The **subject** is that of which something is said.
4. The **predicate** is that which is said of the subject.
5. A sentence may be: **Declarative, Interrogative, Imperative,** or **Exclamatory**.
6. A **declarative sentence** is a sentence that affirms or denies something of the subject; as, *He loves to study. The ship did not sink.*
7. An **imperative sentence** is a sentence that expresses a command; as, *Study your lessons.*
8. An **interrogative sentence** is a sentence that asks a question; as, *Who has a marble?*
9. An **exclamatory sentence** is a sentence that expresses emotion; as, *How well he plays!*

How Sentences should be Written.

10. Begin each sentence with a capital letter.

Place a period (.) at the end of every declarative and imperative sentence.

Place an interrogation-point (?) at the end of every interrogative sentence.

THE SENTENCE.

Place an exclamation-point (!) at the end of every exclamatory sentence.

EXERCISES.

I. WRITE SENTENCES, EACH CONTAINING ONE OF THE FOLLOWING WORDS AS SUBJECT : *horse, dog, cat, fire, water, flower*.

II. WRITE SENTENCES, EACH CONTAINING ONE OF THE FOLLOWING WORDS AS PREDICATE : *runs, swims, flies, walks, jumps, leaps*.

III. POINT OUT THE DECLARATIVE, IMPERATIVE, INTERROGATIVE, AND EXCLAMATORY SENTENCES IN THE FOLLOWING :

George reads. Mary sings. Patrick studies. Hush! it is the dead of night! The bird is on the tree. Go quickly. Study your lessons. Adieu, my native land! Does he write his exercise? Write neatly.

The subject of an imperative sentence is the person spoken to, and is represented by *thou* or *you*.

IV. WRITE FOUR DECLARATIVE SENTENCES, EACH CONTAINING THE WORD *bird*.

EXAMPLE : 1. The *bird* has wings. 2. The *bird* flies.

V. WRITE FOUR IMPERATIVE SENTENCES, EACH CONTAINING THE NAME *Thomas*.

VI. WRITE FOUR INTERROGATIVE SENTENCES, EACH CONTAINING THE WORD *boy*.

VII. WRITE FOUR EXCLAMATORY SENTENCES, EACH CONTAINING THE EXCLAMATION *O*.

COPY THE FOLLOWING SENTENCES, PAYING STRICT ATTENTION TO CAPITALS, SPELLING, AND PUNCTUATION :

Heaven lies about us in our infancy.
The child is father of the man.

Are we to die like slaves?
Go thou and do likewise.
Begone! foul tempter!
Where are you going?
Come one, come all, this rock shall fly
From its firm base as soon as I!
Go where duty calls thee.
Kind words are the music of the world.

II.

THE NOUN.

1. There are over two hundred thousand words in the English language. All these words can be arranged into nine classes, called *parts of speech.*

2. One of these classes is made up of words used as names; as, *Henry* bought me a new *book.*

In this sentence *Henry* and *book* are nouns, because they are names.

3. A **noun** is a word used as a name.

4. A noun may include many things of the same class, when it is called COMMON; as, *man, boy, book.* These words are known as **common nouns**.

5. A **name** may refer to some particular person or place, when it is called PROPER; as, *John, Baltimore, Ireland, America.* These words are known as **proper nouns**.

I. TELL WHETHER THE NOUN IS THE NAME OF A PERSON, AN ANIMAL, A PLACE, OR A THING:

cow	Joseph	lamp	Rome
wood	paper	Buffalo	collar
apple	picture	wagon	chair
brass	table	Michael	desk
flower	Albany	grass	Paul
sheep	dog	squirrel	mouse
Brooklyn	Trenton	iron	glass

The Noun.

II. Tell whether the proper noun indicates the name of a person or a place:

Charles	Lewis	Yonkers	Dublin
London	Berlin	Lawrence	Sarah
James	Mary	Peter	Boston

III. Write the names of:

Five things that you see in the room.
Five things that you have at home.
Five parts of the human body.
Five streets in the city.
Five boys whom you know.
Five girls whom you know.

IV. Fill the blanks with nouns as in the example:
The —— was lost. The *ship* was lost.

1. The —— has fallen. The —— is before the door. The —— comes in through the window.

2. The judge sentenced the ——. The —— fell into the —— and shouted for help.

3. Washington was the first —— of the United States. —— Columbus discovered ——. Cooper wrote many interesting ——.

4. The river freezes in ——. The —— sings sweetly. The —— lost their way in the ——.

V. Insert one or other of the following words before its most appropriate quality, as in example:

stone	tin	water	lemon
candy	rubber	milk	emerald
paste	feathers	glue	garnet
chalk	vinegar	salt	pearls
sponge	flowers	cork	diamonds
glass	cotton	coal	leather

1. *Stone* is heavy. —— is elastic. —— is sticky. —— is red. —— is brittle. —— is sour. —— is white. —— is useful. Lemon is ——. —— is sweet. —— is nourishing. —— is green. —— is soft. —— are light. —— is granular. —— are precious. —— is soft. —— are sweet-smelling. —— is light. —— are precious. —— is transparent. —— is white. —— is black. —— is flexible.

III.

THE ARTICLE.

1. **An article** is a word used to determine the sense in which a noun is taken; as, *the* school; *a* man; *an* eye. A noun may be taken in a definite or in an indefinite sense.

2. There are **two articles**, the **definite** and the **indefinite**.

3. The **definite** article is THE. It points out some particular object or objects; as, *the* man; *the* houses.

4. The **indefinite** article is AN or A. It does not point out any particular object; as, *a* city, *an* envelope.

5. **A** is used before a word beginning with a **consonant** sound; as, *a* stove; *a* yard; *a* unit; *a* well.

6. **An** is used before a word beginning with a vowel sound; as, *an* errand, *an* excuse, *an* urn, *an* hour.

I. SUPPLY THE PROPER ARTICLE WHERE THE DASH OCCURS, AS IN EXAMPLE:

Give *the* boy this slate. Jefferson wrote —— Declaration of Independence. The prize was won by —— little boy. He gathered —— bunch of flowers. —— eagle is in the cage. Give Henry —— orange. More than —— hundred boys were present.

II. —— pagan emperor mourned even —— loss of ——.

day. —— few years that make up our life are of ——
greatest importance. —— good pupil employs —— time
well. —— small leak may sink —— great ship. James
loves —— country. —— autumn strews —— ground with
leaves. Tell —— boy to get —— apples.

III. WHERE THE DASH OCCURS, INSERT ONE OF THE FOL-
LOWING WORDS PRECEDED BY *an* OR *a*:

        1. Honest, youth, union, elm.
        2. Hundred, unit, yoke, hour.

1. *An honest* boy was selected. —— is a promising boy.
—— of the various schools was organized. —— was blown
down last week.

2. —— men were present. —— of oxen are at work.
The number one is ——. —— passes quickly.

IV.

THE ADJECTIVE.

An **adjective** is a word used to qualify or describe a
noun or pronoun; as, a *good* boy; *diligent* men.

In the preceding examples the words *good* and *diligent*
are adjectives, because they are used to qualify or describe
nouns.

I. POINT OUT THE ADJECTIVES IN THE FOLLOWING SEN-
TENCES: Sweet bread. Hard crackers. Warm clothing. A
soft hat. Fine salt. A large kettle. The good boy. A fierce
dog. A generous man. A skilful worker. A busy bee. A
fine house. The largest tree. The beautiful book. An
eloquent speech. A handsome statue. An elegant dress.
A noble mansion.

II. 1. WRITE FIVE SENTENCES, EACH CONTAINING THE
WORD *book*, WITH A DIFFERENT ADJECTIVE QUALIFYING
THE WORD *book*.

2. Write five sentences, each containing the word *house*, with a different adjective qualifying the word *house*.

3. Write five sentences, each containing the word *man*, with a different adjective qualifying the word *man*.

4. Write a list of twenty adjectives.

III. Supply adjectives where the dashes are:

The —— man has gone to England. The —— pupil will learn. The —— man is admired and loved. —— manners are a perpetual letter of recommendation. A —— conscience is above all price. An —— boy is the joy of his parents. Our —— angels continually watch over us. —— prayers are dear to God. The saints are the —— friends of their Heavenly Father. The steeple of the —— church is —— and ——.

V.

THE PRONOUN.

A pronoun is a word that stands for a noun; as, *His* coat; *My* slate; *Who* was here?

In the preceding examples, *his*, *my*, and *who* are pronouns because they stand for nouns.

The principal pronouns are:

I, denoting the speaker.

We, denoting the speaker along with others.

You, denoting one or more persons spoken to.

He, She, It, denoting the person or thing spoken of.

They, denoting the persons or things spoken of.

The personal pronoun *I* should always be a capital letter.

I. Point out the pronouns in the following sentences:

I am pleased with you. We wish you to come with us. Your brother brought my book. Will you give that flower to me? Our new house is finished. He wants me to give it to him. They are to go to Philadelphia. She has gone to the church with him.

II. WRITE THE FOLLOWING SENTENCES, USING PRONOUNS INSTEAD OF NOUNS IN ITALICS:

William and *Charles* went to see George. The teacher told the pupils that the *teacher* would distribute the premiums on Wednesday. The boys went to play after the *boys* had recited their lessons. The girls went to the park after the *girls'* mother had returned home. The pupils came to school, but the *pupils* did not know the *pupils'* lessons.

III. WRITE THE FOLLOWING SENTENCES, REPLACING THE DASH BY A PRONOUN:

Do —— go to Boston? Shall —— go to Washington? Will —— come to the lecture? —— will get the book. —— do our duty. —— will be there in time. All of —— are loved by God. Between you and —— let the matter rest.

VI.

THE VERB.

A **verb** is a word that expresses being, action, or the being acted upon; as, God *is;* The horse *runs;* James *was punished.*

In the examples given, *is* expresses being; *runs* expresses action; and *was punished*, being acted upon.

I. MENTION THE VERBS IN THE FOLLOWING SENTENCES:

God is love. Charity covers a multitude of sins. Perseverance overcomes obstacles. Diligence inspires confidence. Labor conquers all things. God defends the right. Life is short. Prayer is the strength of the soul. The cross is the ladder to Paradise. Union is strength. Humility is the shortest road to perfection. The world is deceitful. President Garfield was shot. Benjamin Harrison was elected President.

II. SUPPLY VERBS IN THE FOLLOWING:

A rolling stone —— no moss. A word —— enough to the wise man. The Lord —— my shepherd. Sloth —— all things difficult. To err —— human. Never buy what you —— not want, because it is cheap. Every man —— the architect of his own fortune. Virtue —— true happiness. Kind hearts —— more than coronets. Alexander Hamilton —— shot. A soft answer —— away anger. Every one —— the son of his own works. A well-spent day —— for us a sweet repose.

III. FORM FIVE SENTENCES, EACH CONTAINING *are*.
" " " " " *is*.
" " " " " *am*.
" " " " " *was*.
" " " " " *were*.
" " " " " *be*.

VII.

THE ADVERB.

An **adverb** is a word used to modify a verb, an adjective, or another adverb; as, You should speak *slowly;* The flower is *exceedingly* beautiful; The sun shines *very brightly*.

In the examples given, *slowly, exceedingly, very,* and *brightly* are adverbs

Slowly modifies the verb *speak* by telling how to speak; *exceedingly* modifies the adjective *beautiful* by showing the degree of beauty; and *very* modifies the adverb *brightly* by telling how *brightly* the sun shines.

I. MENTION THE ADVERBS IN THE FOLLOWING SENTENCES:

Always speak truthfully and act nobly. The day was exceedingly bright. The man acted foolishly. Act well your part. He went to New Mexico yesterday. If you study diligently you will improve. The bird sang sweetly. The more humble we are, the more kindly we will talk. How beautiful is life when it is the way to God! How sweet is death when it is the gate of heaven! Oh! to look upon the face of God eternally, how sweet a destiny!

II. WHERE THE DASH OCCURS INSERT A SUITABLE ADVERB:

Pupils should listen —— and —— to their teacher The boys labored ——, and they gained —— great esteem. Joseph skates —— and ——. The work was done —— and ——. He walked —— to the door and opened it ——. The farmer —— seized his gun and —— attacked the thief. The book was —— interesting, and all listened —— to the reading.

VIII.

THE PREPOSITION.

A **preposition** is a word used to express the relation between its object and a preceding word; as, He went *from* New York *to* Baltimore.

In the example given, the word *from* shows the relation between went and New York; and the word *to* shows the relation between New York and Baltimore.

1. MENTION THE PREPOSITIONS IN THE FOLLOWING SENTENCES:

The smoke is above the city. The paper is around the box. The ship sailed by the city. Put the box on the table. Margaret is at home. They stood between the houses. Take that book to Patrick with my best wishes. Idleness is the devil's fish-hook for catching souls. An idle boy is like an uncultivated field. Learn to be silent sometimes for the edification of others.

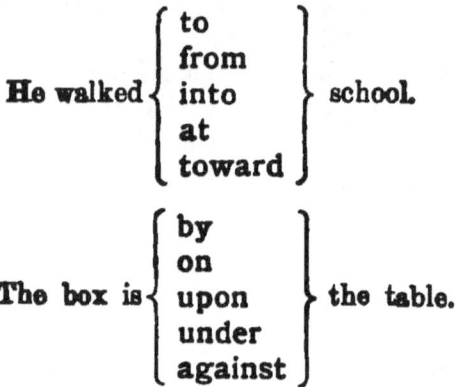

The prepositions within the brackets show the relation between the words they connect.

II. INSERT THE PROPER PREPOSITION WHERE THE DASH OCCURS:

Magellan's ship sailed —— the world. The boy received a book —— his aunt. The Mayflower sailed —— Plymouth. The star rested —— Bethlehem. The lady passed —— the gate —— the city. —— whom are you speaking? The jewels are —— the box. The ways —— God are not man's ways. They walked —— the grove.

IX.

THE CONJUNCTION.

A **conjunction** is a word used to connect words or sentences; as, Charles *and* Matthew are good boys, *but* George is idle.

In the example given *and* and *but* are conjunctions, because the word *and* connects the words Matthew and Charles, and *but* connects the two clauses of the sentence.

(A clause is a sentence forming a part of another sentence.)

I. Point out the conjunctions in the following sentences:

Take care of the cents, and the dollars will take care of themselves. Avoid evil and do good. Be just and fear not. Many are called, but few are chosen. In youth the heart exults and sings. I will return because it looks cloudy. Though he slay me, yet will I trust him. Neither moon nor stars could be seen. Water is much heavier than air. Nothing in life has any meaning, except as it draws us nearer to God and presses us more closely to Him.

II. Insert a conjunction where the dash occurs:

We are God's own creatures, —— God is our only good. We cannot get money —— food. Time —— tide wait for no man. Some people promise —— never pay. He visited London —— Paris in his travels. The book was large —— interesting. Michael Angelo was a poet, an architect, a painter, —— a sculptor. Forgive —— thou shalt be forgiven. Watch —— pray lest you fall into temptation. George walks gracefully —— slowly —— firmly. The bee lays up honey —— it may have food for the winter.

X.

THE INTERJECTION.

1. An interjection is a word that expresses emotion; as, *Lo!* the conquering hero comes!

2. Surprise, joy, contempt, fear, disappointment, and like feelings are called emotions.

In the sentence, Lo! the conquering hero comes! the word *lo* is an interjection.

I. Point out the interjection in the following sentences:

Hark! 'tis the bell of the village church. Oh! how you hurt me! Alas! the poor man is dead. O, he is a cruel boy! O, to pray believingly! Well done, thou good and faithful servant! Pshaw! my book is torn. Welcome! kind friend. Hurrah! we're saved. Bravo! good boy. O sleep, it is a gentle thing!

II. WHERE THE DASH OCCURS INSERT A SUITABLE INTERJECTION.

He came, —— too late. ——, that's nothing. ——, the little maiden said. ——, poor Yorick. -——, be still ——, the bell tolls.

SUMMARY.

The Parts of Speech.

1. **Nouns** and
2. **Pronouns,** } used to *name* persons and things, } are always required to make up a sentence.
3. **Verbs** are used to express being or action.
4. **Articles,**
5. **Adjectives,** and
6. **Adverbs,** } used to modify other words, } may help to form sentences.
7. **Prepositions** and
8. **Conjunctions,** } used to show the connection between other words,
9. **Interjections,** } used to express emotion, } often stand alone.

TELL WHAT KIND OF SENTENCES THE FOLLOWING ARE, AND NAME THE PARTS OF SPEECH:

Patience is a shield that defends us against our afflictions. Everything on earth has an end. Remember thy

Creator in the days of thy youth. The obedient man will speak of victory. O, what a noble science is that of knowing how to love God and save one's soul! Earth is th*e* place to merit heaven. Are they to go to the country to-day? O, foolish boy! Go study your lessons. Send me the man. Alas! they had been friends in youth.

PROPERTIES OF THE NOUN.

1. To the noun belong **gender, person, number,** and **case.** These are called its *properties* or *modifications.*

2. **Person** is that property that distinguishes the speaker or writer, the person or thing addressed, and the person or thing spoken of.

3. There are three persons: the first, the second, and the third.

4. The **first person** denotes the speaker or writer; as, *I, Joseph,* demand it.

5. The **second person** denotes the person or thing addressed; as, *Henry,* will *you* come? Wave *your* tops, *ye* pines.

6. The **third person** denotes the person or thing spoken of; as, *John* and *Joseph* are going to school.

MENTION THE PERSON OF THE NOUN IN THE FOLLOWING SENTENCES:

I, Napoleon, command you. Henry, are you going to New Orleans? Pirates from the Barbary States often attacked our ships. New York was once the capital of the United States. Burgoyne surrendered at Saratoga. I, Charles, will do as you desire. Don't give up the ship. We have met the enemy.

Properties of the Noun.

Number.

7. Number is a *property* or *modification* that distinguishes one thing from more than one.

8. There are **two numbers**, the *singular* and the *plural*.

9. The **singular number** denotes but one thing; as, *pen, cow.*

10. The **plural number** denotes more than one thing; as, *pens, cows.*

11. Most nouns form their plural by adding *s* to the singular form; as, *house, houses; book, books.*

12. Some nouns having a plural form are treated only as nouns in the singular number; as, *alms, mathematics, means, news.*

13. Some nouns are used in the plural only. The most ordinary are: *ashes, bellows, billiards, bowels, measles, scissors.*

14. Nouns whose last syllable will not unite with *s* form their plural by adding *es* to the singular; as, *bush, bushes.*

15. Nouns ending in *y* preceded by a consonant change *y* into *i* and add *es;* as, *army, armies.*

16. Some nouns ending in *f* or *fe* change these endings into *ves* in forming the plural; as, *knife, knives.*

17. Most nouns ending in *o* preceded by a consonant add *es*; as, *cargo, cargoes.*

18. Some nouns form their plural by a change of vowels.

19. A few nouns are alike in both numbers; as, *sheep, deer, swine.*

20. In compound words the plural is formed by making the principal word plural; as, *stepson, stepsons; brother-in-law, brothers-in-law.*

Properties of the Noun. 23

21. Letters, figures, and marks add *'s* or *es* to form their plural; as, *p's, o's, t's, i's,* 1*'s.*

I. Write the following nouns in the plural:

1. patron   heir   fox   fish
   citizen   comrade   tax   echo
   cousin   grotto   lash   potato

II. Write or spell the plural of the nouns:

day   fancy   bag   bounty
navy   duty   Henry   journey
key   balcony   Emily   sky
fly   enemy   boy   study
valley   monkey   penny   beauty

III. Give the Plural of the nouns:

wife   calf   knife   beef
loaf   wharf   dwarf   fife
life   muff   wolf   thief
shelf   gulf   safe   handkerchief

IV. Write or spell the following words in the singular:

teeth   geese   women   skies
mice   matches   ladies   oxen
pianos   children   tomatoes   horses
feet   moneys   armies   peaches

V. Tell whether the following nouns are singular or plural:

wages   rice   thanks   billiards
alms   sugar   scissors   tongs
barley   mathematics   wheat   news
riches   oats   potatoes   pincers
annals   measles   parsley   raisins

VI. Give the plural of the following nouns:

Father-in-law, step-daughter, son-in-law, major-general, daughter-in-law, account-book, lord-justice, woman-servant, deer, salmon.

VII. Fill in the blanks with such of the following words as will complete the sense:

Steel, iron, silver, lead, brass, paper, leather, straw, clay, milk, flour.

Swords are made of ———. Boilers are made of ———. Hats are made of ———. Pipes are made of ———. Cake is made of ———. Watches are made of ———. Bells are made of ———. Books are made of ———. Shoes are made of ———. Cheese is made of ———.

VIII. Write two sentences, each containing a noun in the first person; each containing one or more nouns in the third person.

IX. Write three sentences, each containing one or more nouns in the singular number; also three, each containing one or more nouns in the plural number.

Gender.

22. **Gender** is a property of nouns, which expresses distinction in the names of living beings, and of things without life.

23. There are **three** genders: the masculine, feminine, and neuter.

24. The **masculine gender** is that which denotes the names of males; as, *man, stag*.

25. The **feminine gender** is that which denotes the names of females; as, *woman, cow*.

26. The **neuter gender** is that which denotes the names of things that are neither male nor female; as, *stone, water*.

27. The word *neuter* means *neither*.

Properties of the Noun.

28. Nouns that may be either masculine or feminine are said to be of the **common gender**; as, *parent, child.*

29. The **masculine** and **feminine** of nouns are distinguished in three ways:

I. By the use of different words:

Masculine.	*Feminine.*	*Masculine.*	*Feminine.*
bachelor	maid	king	queen
boy	girl	lad	lass
brother	sister	landlord	landlady
husband	wife	lord	lady
bull	cow	man	woman
drake	duck	master	mistress
father	mother	nephew	niece
monk	nun	papa	mamma
gentleman	lady	sir	madam

II. By the use of suffixes:

Masculine.	*Feminine.*	*Masculine.*	*Feminine.*
abbot	abbess	marquis	marchioness
actor	actress	negro	negress
baron	baroness	patron	patroness
bridegroom	bride	prophet	prophetess
count	countess	prince	princess
czar	czarina	shepherd	shepherdess
duke	duchess	songster	songstress
emperor	empress	tailor	tailoress
hero	heroine	protector	protectress

III. By the composition of words:

Masculine.	*Feminine.*
buck-rabbit	doe-rabbit
he-goat	she-goat
male-child	female-child
man-servant	maid-servant

Properties of the Noun.

30. Things without life are said to be personified when they are spoken to, or spoken of, as persons or living beings; as, *Charity* seeketh not *her* own.

EXERCISES.

I. STATE THE GENDER OF THE FOLLOWING NOUNS:

king	dressmaker	lion	mistress	duck
queen	milliner	hen	house	captain
general	embroiderer	horse	knowledge	nephew

II. STATE THE GENDER OF THE NOUNS IN THE FOLLOWING SENTENCES:

We orphans are deserving of care. The beggar came this morning to the door. The way was long, the wind was cold. The prophet came down from the mountain. The teacher was sick yesterday. My niece is in Europe. Have you seen our old friend?

III. CHANGE INTO THE FEMININE, THE NOUNS THAT ARE ITALICIZED:

The *shepherd* is dead. Is the *lion* fierce? Where is the *bridegroom* this morning? The *tailor* has brought the coat. The *widower* is very poor. The *baron* is reading Callista. The *heir* has succeeded to the estate. The *prophet* is dead. The *lad* has left home. The *bull* has strayed out of the field. The *gentleman* is in the parlor.

IV. CHANGE THE ITALICIZED NOUNS INTO THE MASCULINE:

The *lady* has gone to the library. The *girl* is going to Boston. The *protectress* of the children is dead. The

Properties of the Noun.

princess has married. Her *aunt* is sick. The *empress* has gone to Germany. The *countess* is at the hotel. The *governess* is at home.

Case.

31. **Case** is a mode of inflection showing the relation of nouns or pronouns to some other words in the sentence.

32. There are **three cases**: the nominative, the possessive, and the objective.

33. The nominative and objective cases of nouns are always **the same** in form.

34. The **nominative case** is that form of a noun or pronoun that denotes the subject of a verb; as, *Generosity* gains friends.

35. The subject of a verb is that which answers to the question *who* or *what* before the verb; as, *Generosity gains friends*. What gains friends? *Generosity.* Therefore *generosity* is the subject.

36. The **possessive case** is that form of a noun or a pronoun that denotes the relation of possession; as, the *man's* hat; *my* coat.

37. The possessive case of nouns is formed in the singular by adding an *s* with an apostrophe (') to the nominative form; as, the *bird's* feathers.

38. When the nominative plural ends in *s* the apostrophe alone is added to form the possessive; as, the *ladies'* fans.

39. When the nominative plural does not end in *s*, the possessive case is formed in the same manner as in the singular; as, *children's* toys are dear to them.

40. The **objective case** expresses the object of a verb or of a preposition; as, I heard the *ripple* washing in the *reeds*.

41. The *object* of a verb or a preposition answers to the question *whom* or *what* after it; as, *I heard the ripple washing in the reeds.* I heard *what?* I heard the *ripple* washing in *what?* Washing in the *reeds.* *Ripple* and *reeds* are in the objective case.

Declension.

42. The **declension** of a noun is the naming of a noun in all its cases in both numbers.

EXAMPLES OF DECLENSION.

Singular.	*Plural.*	*Singular.*	*Plural.*
Nom. ox	oxen	*Nom.* sheep	sheep
Poss. ox's	oxen's	*Poss.* sheep's	sheep's
Obj. ox	oxen	*Obj.* sheep	sheep
Nom. man	men	*Nom.* lady	ladies
Poss. man's	men's	*Poss.* lady's	ladies'
Obj. man	men	*Obj.* lady	ladies

EXERCISES.

I. GIVE THE POSSESSIVE FORM TO THE FOLLOWING NOUNS:

1. William, Joseph, Thomas, broker, banker, teacher, mother, sister, army.

2. Judge, sailor, doctor, woman, torches, children, Catherine, scientist, gardener.

II. CHANGE THE PHRASES IN ITALICS INTO NOUNS IN THE POSSESSIVE CASE:

The *marbles of the boy* are in the drawer. He came to

do *the will of his father.* I found in the street *the book belonging to Ann.* The *tools of the carpenters* are in the tool-chest. The *hat of the lady* is trimmed with an ostrich feather. It is *the journey of a day* between the two towns.

III. MENTION THE CASE OF THE NOUNS IN THE FOLLOWING SENTENCES:

Grammar is an important study. Wordsworth is the most correct writer of modern poets. His home is on the deep. We left him alone with his glory. Cardinal Newman wrote classic English prose. The end of government is the good of mankind. Write your address on your slate.

IV. WHERE THE DASH OCCURS INSERT A NOUN IN THE PROPER CASE THAT WILL COMPLETE THE SENSE:

Health, girl, day, patriot, Turk, children, evening, Indian, work.

Edward Everett was a celebrated orator. Temperance promotes ——. The morning star, the harbinger of ——. Isabel saw a tear standing in the —— eye. The —— blood was shed in a noble cause. Bring me —— hat. Great —— are wrought by prayer. The —— was warm. The —— was dreaming of the hour. The —— was captured by the ——.

V. WHERE THE DASH OCCURS INSERT A NOUN THAT WILL COMPLETE THE SENSE:

    1. Bird, clock, soldier, boy, pony.
    2. Musician, straw, knowledge, hope.
    3. Snow, fire, squirrel, songs.

1. The wind was bitterly cold. How sweetly the ―― sings! Does the ―― like to skate? The old ―― spoke the truth. The wooden ―― is stopped. The ―― ran away.

2. ―― played on the harp. We acquire ―― by patient study. While ―― remains there can be no positive misery. A ―― will furnish an occasion when people are determined to quarrel.

3. The ―― covered the ground. The merry little ―― sat quietly on the branch. The ―― burns cheerily. He sang sweetly the old ―― of his boyhood.

VI. PARSE THE NOUNS IN THE FOLLOWING SENTENCES, AS IN THE EXAMPLES:

Thomas lost Mary's book.

Thomas is a noun because it is a name; it is a proper noun because it is the name of a particular individual; in the third person because it is spoken of; in the singular number because it denotes but one; of the masculine gender because it denotes a person of the male sex; in the nominative case because it is the subject of the verb lost.

Mary's is a noun (*why?*); it is a proper noun (*why?*); in the third person (*why?*); in the singular number (*why?*); in the feminine gender (*why?*); in the possessive case because it denotes the relation of possession.

Book is a common noun (*why?*); of the third person (*why?*); singular number (*why?*); neuter gender (*why?*); and objective case because it denotes the object of the verb lost.

George has found the grocer's boat. The tapers gleamed from the altar. Bright visions came to me. The curfew tolls the knell of parting day. When you are tempted, have recourse to prayer. Eternal life's a precious good. Sin makes death terrible. Joseph lost his father's razor. The children's toys were easily broken. We are always in God's presence.

VII. WRITE FIVE SENTENCES, EACH CONTAINING A NOUN IN THE NOMINATIVE CASE.

VIII. WRITE THREE SENTENCES, EACH CONTAINING A NOUN IN THE POSSESSIVE CASE.

IX. WRITE THREE SENTENCES, EACH CONTAINING A NOUN IN THE OBJECTIVE CASE.

X. WRITE SENTENCES, EACH CONTAINING ONE OR MORE OF THE FOLLOWING WORDS:

tree	eye	father's	knife
house	desk	brother's	floor
park	seats	parents	railing
coat	ships	watch	steps

Syntax of the Noun.

1. A noun that is the subject of a verb must be in the nominative case; as, Honesty is the best policy.
2. A noun in the possessive case is governed by the name of the thing possessed; as, I have Peter's slate.
3. A noun used as an attribute is put in the same case as the word to which it belongs; as, John is a good boy.
4. A noun used to explain a noun or pronoun going before is in the same case; as, Henry, the gardener, is sick.

ADJECTIVES.

Classes of Adjectives.

1. An **adjective** is a word used to qualify or describe a noun or pronoun; as, a *good* school; *fine, diligent* boys; he is *strong*.

2. Adjectives are divided into **five classes**: common, proper, numeral, pronominal, and participial.

3. A **common adjective** is a word that expresses quality, quantity, or place; as, *good, bad, little, much, eastern, outer*.

4. A **proper adjective** is one derived from a proper name; as, the *American* flag; the *Irish* cause; the *Canadian* people.

5. A **numeral adjective** is one that expresses a definite number; as, *two* pears; the *second* boy; a *single* book.

6. Numeral adjectives are of three kinds: cardinal, ordinal, multiplicative.

(1) The **cardinal adjective** tells how many; as, *one, two*.

(2) The **ordinal adjective** tells which one; as, *first, second*.

(3) The **multiplicative adjective** tells how many fold; as, *single* or *alone*; *double* or *twofold*.

7. A **pronominal adjective** is an adjective that performs the office of certain pronouns; that is, it may be used with a noun or represent a noun.

8. The principal pronominal adjectives are: *all, another, any; both, each, either, enough, every, few; former, latter; little, less, least; much, more, most, many; none, neither, one, other, some, several, same, such*.

ADJECTIVES.

9. **A participial adjective** is an adjective derived from a verb and having the form of a participle; as, a *loving* mother; the *rising* sun.

EXERCISES.

I. WHERE THE DASH OCCURS INSERT A SUITABLE ADJECTIVE TAKEN FROM THE LIST:

1. Large, beautiful, wooden, small, walnut, wonderful.
2. Industrious, eminent, spacious, elegant, ordinary, useless.

1. A —— house. A —— sight. A —— bowl. A —— tree. A —— table. A —— sight.
2. An —— man. The —— surgeon. A —— hall. An —— apartment. An —— occurrence. A —— task.

II. POINT OUT THE ADJECTIVES AND ARTICLES IN THE FOLLOWING SENTENCES:

The day is cold and dark and dreary. His hair is crisp and black and long. Great, wide, beautiful, and wonderful world. The brave, kind, noble boy was rewarded. The fruit is large, rich, and ripe. She is an agreeable, obedient, respectful, and good-hearted girl. The pupils are neither rude nor ugly. Strive to be useful and contented. He is a pale, slim, delicate boy. The wooden house has a slanting roof.

III. MENTION WHETHER THE FOLLOWING ADJECTIVES ARE PROPER OR COMMON:

sweet	cheerful	bright	narrow
stormy	Spanish	pretty	late
proud	wealthy	high	useful
English	Grecian	Italian	fine

IV. Mention six pronominal adjectives, and write sentences, each containing one.

V. Insert one or more of the following numeral or pronominal adjectives that will complete the sense in the following sentences:

Each, all, once, former, none, later, some, one, other, such, twenty.

They had —— an apple. He spoke —— time after being struck. The —— book has a large sale, the —— but little. The —— went to the field, the —— remained. The boat is the —— that was used yesterday. —— of the man rode a gray horse, the —— a black one. The punishment was —— as he deserved. The cows were in the barn.

VI. Point out the numeral and pronominal adjectives in the following sentences:

Every boy will be expected to do his duty. All men must die. Each of the scholars received a prize. Neither of us is to blame. He took a twofold view of the subject. Four boys want the second book. The first telegraphic message was sent in 1844. James Monroe was fifth President of the United States, and served two terms.

VII. Parse the adjectives in the sentences here given according to the two following examples:

Example I. *All good books are interesting companions.*

All is a pronominal adjective, because it shows in what sense the noun *books* is taken.

Good is a common adjective, because it qualifies the noun *books*.

ADJECTIVES. 35

Interesting is a participial adjective, because it has the form of a participle and qualifies the noun *companions*.

EXAMPLE II. *Two of my schoolmates won prizes in the French language.*

Two is a numeral adjective, because it expresses number.

French is a proper adjective, because it is derived from a proper name.

The explorers of the Mississippi valley were mostly Jesuit priests. The first permanent English settlement was made at Jamestown. The same amount of work was exacted from each. He is an able, intelligent, and cultured scientist, and occupies an eminent position. They are distinguished people and lead virtuous lives. Longfellow was a famous American poet.

Comparison of Adjectives.

10. Comparison is a change in the form of an adjective to express different degrees of quality or quantity; as, *hard, harder, hardest; soft, softer, softest.*

11. The **degrees** of comparison are three in number: the positive, the comparative, and the superlative.

12. The **positive degree** is expressed by the adjective in its simplest form; as, *wide, great.*

13. The **comparative degree** is expressed by adding *r* or *er* to the positive; as, *wider, greater.*

14. The **superlative degree** is expressed by adding *st* or *est* to the positive; as, *widest, greatest.*

REGULAR COMPARISON.

15. The comparatives of adjectives of one syllable are commonly formed by adding *er* to the positive; and the superlatives, by adding *est;* as, *great, greater, greatest.*

ADJECTIVES.

16. Degrees of comparison may also be expressed by adding the adverbs **more** and **most** to the adjective; as, gay, *more* gay, *most* gay.

17. Adjectives of more than one syllable are generally compared by means of the adverbs **more** and **most**; as, useful, *more* useful, *most* useful.

18. The degrees of diminution are expressed by the adverbs **less** and **least**; as, noble, *less* noble, *least* noble.

19. Those adjectives whose signification does not admit of different degrees cannot be compared; as, *two, all, infinite, supreme, universal, eternal.*

EXERCISES.

I. COMPARE THE FOLLOWING ADJECTIVES:

Positive.	*Comparative.*	*Superlative.*
sharp,	———,	———.
long,	———,	———.
high,	———,	———.
broad,	———,	———.
old,	———,	———.
small,	———,	———.
short,	———,	———.
deep,	———,	———.
light,	———,	———.
cool,	———,	———.

II. INSERT IN THE FOLLOWING SENTENCES ONE OR OTHER OF THE WORDS HERE GIVEN:

Gentle, clear, stronger, wise, honest, tough, kind, dull, healthy.

ADJECTIVES. 37

He is a very —— boy. —— meat was given away. The parents were exceedingly ——. He possesses a —— and vigorous mind. The —— boy will be mindful of little things. The —— man neglects his business. George is —— than his brother. The —— sailor has a —— appearance.

III. MAKE A LIST OF TWELVE ADJECTIVES.

IV. PARSE THE ADJECTIVES IN THE FOLLOWING SENTENCES:

Coals are black. Fresh water was on the table. A beautiful, large, black cat lay on the rug before the fire. The Church is the pillar and ground of truth. An innocent child is a fragrant flower in the garden of the Lord. Always give good example.

Syntax of the Adjective.

The *comparative degree* should be used only in reference to two persons or things; as, John is taller than William.

The *superlative degree* compares one or more with all others of the same kind; as, Theodore is the tallest boy in class.

The expression *each other* should be applied to only two objects; *one another* to more than two. Examples: These two boys assist each other. Christians should assist one another.

Either and *neither* relate to two things only; as, The teacher said that neither Mary nor Ellen was right. Either John or Frederick has my knife.

Some relates to more than two things. Some boys and girls study their lessons well.

The pronoun *them* should not be used for the adjective *those*. Do not say, " Give me *them* books," but say, "Give me *those* books."

An *adverb* should not be used instead of an adjective. Do not say, " The water feels *coldly*," but say, " The water feels cold."

PRONOUNS.

1. **A pronoun** is a word that stands for a noun ; as, *his* slate ; *my* hat ; *who* is afraid ?

2. Pronouns are divided into **four classes** ; namely, personal, relative, demonstrative, and interrogative.

Personal Pronouns.

3. **A personal pronoun** is a pronoun that by its form distinguishes the speaker, the person spoken to, and the person or thing spoken of.

4. Personal pronouns are divided into two classes ; namely, simple and compound.

5. The **simple personal pronouns** are five: *I*, of the first person ; *thou*, of the second person; *he, she,* and *it,* of the third person.

6. The **compound personal pronouns** are also five: *myself*, of the first person ; *thyself*, of the second person ; *himself, herself,* and *itself,* of the third person.

7. These pronouns are formed by the addition of the word *self* to the possessive case of the first and second persons and the objective case of the third person.

PRONOUNS.

Declension of the Simple Personal Pronouns

FIRST PERSON.

	Singular.	Plural.
Nom.	I,	we.
Poss.	my or mine,	our or ours.
Obj.	me,	us.

SECOND PERSON.

	Singular.	Plural.
Nom.	thou,	ye or you.
Poss.	thy or thine,	your or yours.
Obj.	thee,	you.

THIRD PERSON.

	Singular.			Plural.
	MASCULINE.	FEMININE.	NEUTER.	
Nom.	he,	she,	it,	they.
Poss.	his,	her or hers,	its,	their or theirs
Obj.	him,	her,	it,	them.

INSERT THE PROPER PRONOUN TO COMPLETE THE SENSE:

—— are going to Rome. —— book was found. This hat is ——. Mary wrote things that are ——. —— are in trouble. —— house has been sold. The cattle are ——. The Lord will reward or punish —— according to our works. All my desires are before ——. —— spoke to —— of —— trials. —— has gone to see —— sister. —— desired to sell —— property.

Relative Pronouns.

8. A **relative pronoun** is a pronoun that relates to a word or phrase going before; as, The man of business *who* wishes to succeed, must labor.

9. A relative pronoun also connects different clauses of a sentence; as, I paid for the goods *which* were sent to me.

10. The word, phrase, or clause to which a pronoun relates is called an **antecedent**.

11. The **simple relative pronouns** are *who, which, what,* and *that*.

12. *Who* is applied to persons; *which,* to animals and things; *that,* to persons and things; *what,* to things.

13. A relative is of the **same** person, number, and gender as its antecedent.

Declension of Who.

Singular and *Plural.* { *Nom.* who,
Poss. whose,
Obj. whom.

Declension of Which.

Singular and *Plural.* { *Nom.* which,
Poss. whose,
Obj. which.

14. *What* and *that* have no declension.

15. The compound relative pronouns are formed by adding *ever* or *soever* to *who, which, what.*

PRONOUNS.

EXERCISES.

SUPPLY THE BLANKS WITH PROPER RELATIVE PRONOUNS:

This is the picture —— I bought yesterday. Who —— has any sense of justice would act differently? He —— is wise will study. I lost the ticket —— you sent. General Grant, —— was a celebrated general, died greatly lamented. The man repeated —— was said. Avoid rudeness of manners, —— always hurts the feelings of others. Here is a man —— promise is to be relied upon. He could not tell —— had befallen him. This is the boat in —— he sailed.

Demonstrative Pronouns.

16. **A demonstrative pronoun** points out the noun with which it is used; as, *This book is mine.* In the example given *this* is a demonstrative pronoun pointing out the noun *book.*

17. The demonstratives are two: **this** and **that**; their plurals, **these** and **those.**

18. The office of the demonstratives is simply to name ;. point out.

19. **This** is always a demonstrative. **That** is used as a conjunction, a demonstrative, and a relative.

EXERCISES.

INSERT DEMONSTRATIVE PRONOUNS WHERE THE DASHES OCCUR:

Where are —— keys? Give me —— flower. Take —— seat. What has happened to —— gentleman? Where is —— picture you bought? Please to buy me —— slate.

Interrogative Pronouns.

20. An **interrogative** pronoun is a pronoun employed in asking questions.

21. **Who, which,** and **what** when used in asking questions are called interrogative pronouns; as, *Who* did this? *Which* is the book? *What* do you want?

22. *Who* is applied to persons; *which,* to persons and things; *what,* to persons and things.

I. INSERT THE PROPER INTERROGATIVE PRONOUNS WHERE THE DASH OCCURS:

—— are you doing? —— do you take? —— party was defeated? In —— steamer do you sail? In —— house do you live? In —— field do you play ball?

II. WRITE OUT THE FOLLOWING SENTENCES, AND DRAW **one** LINE UNDER THE PERSONAL PRONOUNS OF THE SINGULAR NUMBER, AND **two** LINES UNDER THOSE OF THE PLURAL NUMBER:

You are all doing well. He has an excellent character. We are going to the market. She is an amiable girl. It is a beautiful work. They listened with great attention. My brother goes to confession regularly. Does he read well? They are good boys.

III. REPLACE THE DASH BY A PERSONAL PRONOUN:

The ostrich is a bird, but —— cannot fly. Spring has put on —— mantle of green. Give —— a seat. Send for —— mother. —— are to go to Florida. Tell —— to come in. He is one of ——.

Pronouns.

IV. Insert an interrogative pronoun that will complete the sense:

—— discovered America? —— founded the Order of the Brothers of the Christian Schools? —— was the first Christian Martyr? —— book did you get from the library? —— lectured last night? —— was the subject? —— section was most attentive? In —— bank did he deposit his money? In —— city does he live? —— is his hat?

V. Insert the pronouns that the sense requires:

—— will be elected. Shall —— go with ——? Where shall —— learn ——? This is —— the principal approves. Thomas Jefferson, —— wrote the Declaration of Independence, was elected third President of the United States. Out of the depths have —— cried unto ——. She —— was there. I —— spoke to ——. What music have —— heard?

VI. Parse the pronouns in the following sentences:

I wrote to him. The boy who studies will learn. Whose knife is this? John's. I know what is wanted.

I is a pronoun (*why?*); it is a simple personal pronoun (*why?*); of the first person, singular number (*why?*); of the masculine or feminine gender (*why?*); in the nominative case because it is the subject of the verb *wrote*.

Him is a simple personal pronoun (*why?*); of the third person, singular number (*why?*); of the masculine gender (*why?*); in the objective case because it is the object of the preposition *to*.

Who is a simple relative pronoun (*why?*); of the third person, singular number (*why?*); of the masculine gender (*why?*); nominative case because it is the subject of the verb *studies*.

Whose is an interrogative pronoun (*why?*); it is of the third person, singular number (*why?*); of the neuter gender (*why?*); and in the possessive case because it denotes the relation of possession.

What is a relative pronoun, third person, singular number, neuter gender, nominative case to the verb *is wanted*.

VII. NAME AND PARSE THE NOUNS, ARTICLES, ADJECTIVES, AND PRONOUNS IN THE FOLLOWING SENTENCES:

The gentle stranger spoke of his early life. The sincere man is a valuable friend. They are anxious to find him. He has travelled over the American continent. Which of you will go with me? A beautiful chain and an elegant book were given to me.

Syntax of the Pronoun.

1. A pronoun used to explain a noun or pronoun going before is put in the same case. Do not say, "I have seen the boy, *he* that gave me this book," instead of "*him* that gave me this book."

2. A pronoun must agree with the noun or pronoun it represents, in person, number, and gender; as, Our father and mother are here. John has seen *them*.

3. The relative pronouns should be placed as near as possible to the antecedent. Do not say, "We sell hats to men that cost as low as one dollar," instead of "We sell men hats that cost as low as one dollar."

4. When the antecedent is a collective noun, the pronoun representing it must be in the plural number; as, The committee were divided in *their* sentiments.

5. When a pronoun has two or more antecedents con-

nected by *and*, it must agree with them in the plural number; as, Tobias and Noah speak well of *their* friends.

ANALYSIS OF SENTENCES.

1. **Analysis,** in grammar, is the separation of a sentence into its parts.

2. A sentence may be **simple, compound,** or **complex.**

3. A **simple sentence** is a sentence that contains but one proposition; as, *A boy's conduct is a good indication of his character.*

4. A sentence may have two or more subjects and a simple predicate ; or two or more predicates and a simple subject ; as, *Time and tide wait for no man ; The season came and went.*

5. A **compound sentence** is a sentence composed of two or more independent propositions; as, *Industry will be rewarded, but idleness will be punished.*

6. A **complex sentence** is a sentence containing at least two propositions, one of which is principal and the other subordinate; as, *When the sun shines, the boys play.*

7. A **clause** is a sentence forming a part of a compound or complex sentence.

EXERCISES.

I. Unite the following sentences into sentences having compound subjects:

John sings. Thomas sings. Mary reads. Margaret reads. George swims. Francis swims.

{ Ducks swim.
  Geese swim.
  Swans swim.

{ Spears are made of silver.
  Knives are made of silver.
  Forks are made of silver.

Analysis of Sentences.

II. Unite the following sentences within braces into sentences having compound predicates:

{ James can run.   { The men shouted.   { The winter came.
{ James can jump. { The men fell.   { The winter went.

{ Glass is transparent.   { Iron is hard.
{ Glass is brittle.   { Iron is ductile.
{ Glass is smooth.   { Iron is heavy.

III. Unite the following simple sentences so as to form compound sentences:

{ Sleep is the restorer of our strength.
{ Sleep prepares us for a new day's work.

{ The eye is the organ of sight.
{ The eye lies exposed to external impressions.

{ Good books promote the advance of civilization.
{ Goods books are interesting companions.
{ Good books are useful in advancing our mental and religious welfare.

Unite the following clauses so as to form complex sentences:

The man will succeed   The boy was found
Who labors diligently.   That had been lost.

General Grant was a celebrated General
Who was elected president.

I will honor them   The picture was once mine
That honor me.   That you bought.

Who can love the boy   He will win the race
That is continually doing evil? Who is diligent.

Principal Parts of a Sentence.

8. Every sentence must contain two essential parts: the subject and the predicate.

9. **Adjuncts** modify or limit the sense of the principal words in a sentence.

10. Adjuncts are divided into three classes: adjective, adverbial, explanatory.

11. An **adjective adjunct** is an adjunct that is used as an adjective; as, The *diligent* scholar improves.

12. An **adverbial adjunct** is an adjunct used as an adverb; as, He ran *rapidly*.

13. An **explanatory adjunct** is an adjunct used to explain a preceding noun or pronoun; as, My friend, *Joseph*, is well.

14. When the subject is a single word it is called a **simple subject.**

15. The subject with all its modifying words is called the **logical subject**; as, *A thing of beauty* is a joy forever.

16. The **subject** of a sentence may be a noun, a pronoun, a verb in the infinitive mood, a phrase, or a clause.

17. In **imperative sentences** the subject *thou* or *you* is usually understood.

18. When the predicate is simply the verb it is called the **grammatical predicate.**

19. The **logical predicate** includes the verb, with all its adjuncts.

20. Besides a subject and predicate, a sentence usually contains an *object* or an *attribute*. The **object** of a sentence is that in which the action of the transitive verb terminates.

21. The **object** of a sentence may be a noun, a pronoun, a verb, a participle, or a proposition.

22. The **attribute** of a sentence is a word completing the predicate and relating to the subject; as, The flowers are *beautiful.*

23. The attribute of a sentence may be an adjective, a noun, a pronoun, a participle, a verb in the infinitive mood, a phrase, or a clause.

Phrases.

24. A **phrase** is any group of words not containing a verb and its subject, and performing the office of a single word.

25. A phrase that performs the office of an adjective is an **adjective phrase**; one that performs the office of an adverb is called an **adverbial phrase**; and one that performs the office of a noun is called a **noun** or **substantive phrase.**

26. An **explanatory phrase** is a phrase that explains some other word or phrase in a sentence; as, Lew Wallace, *the author of "Ben Hur,"* was American Minister to Constantinople.

27. An **independent phrase** is a phrase that has no grammatical connection with any other word in the sentence; as, *To be candid,* I was in fault.

29. Phrases are divided into simple, complex, and compound.

EXAMPLES FOR ANALYSIS.

Simple Sentences.

EXAMPLE 1. *Boys play.*

This is a simple declarative sentence. It is *simple* because it contains but one proposition; *declarative* because it expresses an affirmation. *Boys* is the subject, because it is that of which the sentence treats. *Play* is the predicate, because it is that which is said of the subject.

I. ANALYZE THE FOLLOWING SENTENCES AS IN THE FOREGOING EXAMPLE:

Men talk.
Students learn.
Children cry.
Time flies.

Birds sing.
Horses gallop.
Dogs bark.
Lions roar.

EXAMPLE 2. *Fire melts gold.*

This is a simple declarative sentence. The subject is *fire;* the predicate, *melts;* the object, *gold.*

II. ANALYZE THE FOLLOWING SENTENCES AS IN THE PRECEDING EXAMPLE:

1. God loves us.
2. Brutus stabbed Cæsar.
3. William defeated Harold.
4. John bought peaches.
5. Generosity makes friends.
6. I have pens.
7. Integrity inspires confidence.
8. Familiarity breeds contempt.

EXAMPLE 3. *Feathers are light.*

This is a simple declarative sentence. The subject is *feathers;* the predicate, *are;* and the attribute is *light.*

III. ANALYZE THE FOLLOWING SENTENCES AS IN THE EXAMPLE:

1. Lead is heavy.
2. Gold is yellow.
3. Stars are suns.

1. Knowledge is power.
5. Resting is rusting.
6. Diamonds are combustible.

EXAMPLE 4. *The old wooden clock stopped.*

This is a simple declarative sentence. The subject is *clock;* the predicate is *stopped.* The subject is limited by the article *the,* and modified by the adjective adjuncts *old* and *wooden.*

IV. ANALYZE THE FOLLOWING SENTENCES AS IN EXAMPLE 4:

The young speaker was applauded. The wooden house fell. The large steamer sank. An honest man prospers. The little child slept. The dark cloud lowers.

EXAMPLE 5. *The full moon sometimes shines brightly.*

This is a simple declarative sentence. The subject is *moon;* the predicate is *shines.* The subject is limited by the article *the,* and modified by the adjective adjunct *full;* the predicate is modified by the adverbial adjuncts *sometimes* and *brightly.*

V. ANALYZE THE FOLLOWING SENTENCES AS IN EXAMPLE 5:

The south wind blew softly. Industrious people rise early. The strong wind changed suddenly. All those various questions may be settled peacefully. The dark, threatening clouds were soon dispersed. Your venerable father will be cordially welcomed.

VERBS.

1. A **verb** is a word that expresses being, action, or the being acted upon; as, John *is* here. The horse *runs.* James *was punished.*

2. Verbs may be classified as regards their **form** and as regards their **meaning**.

3. A **finite verb** is a verb in any other mood than the infinitive.

4. Verbs are divided with respect to their **form** into three classes: **regular, irregular,** and **defective.**

5. A **regular verb** is a verb that forms its imperfect tense and perfect participle by adding *d* or *ed* to the root; as, *reap, reaped; wish, wished.*

6. An **irregular verb** is a verb that does not form its imperfect tense and perfect participle by the addition of *d* or *ed* to its root; as, *know, knew, known.*

7. A **defective verb** is a verb that forms no participles and is not used in all the moods and tenses; as, *can, would.*

POINT OUT THE VERBS THAT EXPRESS BEING OF THE SUBJECT; THOSE THAT EXPRESS ACTION OF THE SUBJECT; AND THOSE THAT EXPRESS THE SUBJECT AS BEING ACTED UPON:

The sun shines. Water flows. Lilies are in the pond. George is in the field. Mary was struck. He sleeps. The pitcher was broken. Henry is honest.

Classification of Verbs.

AS TO THEIR MEANING.

8. Verbs are divided as regards their **meaning** into two classes: **transitive,** and **intransitive.**

9. A **transitive verb** is a verb that expresses action communicated from a subject to an object; as, The boy *reads* the book.

10. An **intransitive verb** is a verb that expresses being,

or state, or action not communicated to an object; as, John *awakes;* George *walks.*

POINT OUT THE TRANSITIVE AND INTRANSITIVE VERBS IN THE FOLLOWING SENTENCES:

Birds build nests. Homer was a poet. The prisoner was released. They eat on the train. The horse was lost. It snows. It appears so to me.

Modifications of Verbs.

11. Verbs have five kinds of modifications or inflections: voice, mood, tense, person, and number.

Voice.

12. **Voice** is a modification of transitive verbs which distinguishes their subject as acting or as being acted upon.
13. There two voices: the active and the passive.

The **active voice** is that form of a transitive verb representing the subject as acting upon the object; as, Wolfe *defeated* Montcalm.

14. The **passive voice** is that form of a transitive verb which represents the subject as being acted upon; as, Montcalm *was defeated* by Wolfe.
15. That which was the object of the verb in the **active voice** becomes its subject in the **passive voice.**

CHANGE THE VERBS IN THE ACTIVE VOICE IN THE FOLLOWING SENTENCES TO VERBS IN THE PASSIVE VOICE:

The Duke of Wellington defeated Napoleon. The Continental soldiers captured Major André. Ethan Allen took

VERBS.

Ticonderoga. Captain John Smith explored the New England coast. The English captured Philadelphia.

Moods.

16. Mood (or **Mode**) is that modification which shows the manner in which the verb asserts something of its subject.

17. There are **five moods**; namely, the infinitive, the indicative, the potential, the subjunctive, and the imperative.

18. The **infinitive mood** is used to express action or being without limitation of person or number; as, I came *to see* him.

19. The **indicative mood** is used to express a direct assertion or ask a direct question; as, John *is* there. *Is* John there?

20. The **potential mood** is used to express possibility, liberty, obligation, or necesssity; as, Men *may* come.

21. The **subjunctive mood** expresses what is doubtful, supposed, or dependent; as, I would go *if* I were you.

22. The **imperative mood** expresses command, entreaty, desire, request, or exhortation; as, *Arise, go forth* and *conquer* as of old.

WRITE TWO SENTENCES, EACH CONTAINING:

A verb in the infinitive mood; a verb in the indicative mood; a verb in the potential mood; a verb in the subjunctive mood; a verb in the imperative mood.

Tense.

23. Tense is a modification of the verb which distinguishes the time of the action or state of being.

24. There are **six tenses**: the present, the imperfect, the perfect, the pluperfect, the future, and the future perfect.

25. The **present tense** is that form of the verb that expresses present time; as, He *is* here. The girl *speaks*.

26. The **imperfect tense** is that form of the verb that expresses action or state of being either completed or continuing in a past time; as, I *wrote* a letter. I *was speaking*.

27. The **perfect tense** expresses action or state of being as completed within the present time; as, I *have written* a letter this morning.

28. The **pluperfect tense** expresses action or state of being as completed at or before some specified time; as, I *had written* this page when he arrived.

29. The **future tense** expresses action or state of being in some time to come; as, I *shall go* to-night.

30. The **future perfect tense** expresses action or state of being as about to be completed at or before a specified future time; as, I *shall have written* my letter by noon.

WRITE FIVE SENTENCES, EACH CONTAINING:

A verb in the present tense; a verb in the imperfect tense; a verb in the perfect tense; a verb in the pluperfect tense; a verb in the future tense; a verb in the future perfect tense.

Conjugation of Verbs.

31. **Four principal parts** enter into the conjugation of every complete verb; namely, the **present**, the **imperfect**, the **imperfect participle**, and the **perfect participle**.

32. These are called the principal parts, because from

them and by means of them all the other parts of the verb are formed.

33. An **auxiliary verb** is a verb that aids in the conjugation of other verbs.

34. The auxiliaries are *do, be, have, shall, will, may, can, must, might, could, would,* and *should.*

35. The auxiliaries *do, be, have, will* are often used as **principal verbs.**

WRITE THREE SENTENCES, EACH CONTAINING:

The auxiliary verb *shall;* the auxiliary verb *will;* the auxiliary verb *may;* the auxiliary verb *can;* the auxiliary verb *must.*

Conjugation of the verb HAVE.

PRINCIPAL PARTS.

Present.	*Imperfect.*	*Imperfect Participle.*	*Perfect Participle.*
have,	**had,**	**having,**	**had.**

Infinitive Mood.

Present Tense.	*Perfect Tense.*
To have,	To have had.

Indicative Mood.

Present Tense.

Sing. 1. I have,
2. Thou hast,
3. He has.

Plur. 1. We have,
2. Ye *or* you have,
3. They have.

VERBS.

Imperfect Tense.

Sing. 1. I had, Plur. 1. We had,
2. Thou hadst, 2. You had,
3. He had. 3. They had.

Perfect Tense.

Sign: **have.**

Sing. 1. I have had, Plur. 1. We have had,
2. Thou hast had, 2. You have had,
3. He has had. 3. They have had.

Pluperfect Tense.

Sign: **had.**

Sing. 1. I had had, Plur. 1. We had had,
2. Thou hadst had, 2. You had had,
3. He had had. 3. They had had.

Future Tense.

Sign: **shall** or **will.**

Sing. 1. I shall have, Plur. 1. We shall have,
2. Thou wilt have, 2. You will have,
3. He will have. 3. They will have.

VERBS.

Future Perfect Tense.

Sign : shall have or will have.

Sing. 1. I shall have had,   *Plur.* 1. We shall have had,
2. Thou wilt have had,   2. You will have had,
3. He will have had.   3. They will have had.

WRITE TWO SENTENCES, EACH CONTAINING:

A verb in the indicative mood imperfect tense ; a verb in the future tense ; a verb in the future perfect tense.

Potential Mood.

Present Tense.

Sign: may, can, or must.

Sing. 1. I may have,   *Plur.* 1. We may have,
2. Thou mayst have,   2. You may have,
3. He may have.   3. They may have.

Imperfect Tense.

Sign: might, could, would, or should.

Sing. 1. I might have,   *Plur.* 1. We might have,
2. Thou mightst have,   2. You might have,
3. He might have.   3. They might have.

Perfect Tense.

Sign : **may, can,** or **must have.**

Sing. 1. I may have had, *Plur.* 1. We may have had,
2. Thou mayst have had,   2. You may have had,
3. He may have had.   3. They may have had

Pluperfect Tense.

Sign: **might, could, would,** or **should have.**

Sing. 1. I might have had, *Plur.* 1. We might have had,
2. Thou mightst have had,   2. You might have had,
3. He might have had.   3. They might have had.

Subjunctive Mood.

Present Tense.

Sing. 1. If I have,   *Plur.* 1. If we have,
2. If thou have,   2. If you have,
3. If he have.   3. If they have.

Imperfect Tense.

Sing. 1. If I had,   *Plur.* 1. If we had,
2. If thou hadst,   2. If you had,
3. If he had.   3. If they had.

Imperative Mood.

Present Tense.

Sing. 2. Have thou, *or* do thou have. *Plur.* 2. Have you, *or* do you have.

PARTICIPLES.

Imperfect. *Perfect.* *Preperfect.*
having, **had.** **having had.**

WRITE OUT TWO SENTENCES, EACH CONTAINING:

A verb in the potential mood, present tense ; a verb in the potential mood, imperfect tense ; a verb in the potential mood, perfect tense ; a verb in the potential mood, pluperfect tense ; a verb in the subjunctive mood, present tense.

Conjugation of the verb BE.

PRINCIPAL PARTS.

Present. *Imperfect.* *Imperfect Participle.* *Perfect Participle.*
be, **was,** **being,** **been.**

Infinitive Mood.

Present Tense. *Perfect Tense.*
To be. To have been.

Verbs.

Indicative Mood.

Present Tense.

Sing. 1. I am,   Plur. 1. We are,
      2. Thou art,   2. You are,
      3. He is.   3. They are.

Imperfect Tense.

Sing. 1. I was,   Plur. 1. We were,
      2. Thou wast *or* wert,   2. You were,
      3. He was.   3. They were.

Perfect Tense.

Sing. 1. I have been,   Plur. 1. We have been,
      2. Thou hast been,   2. You have been,
      3. He has been.   3. They have been.

Pluperfect Tense.

Sing. 1. I had been,   Plur. 1. We had been,
      2. Thou hadst been,   2. You had been,
      3. He had been.   3. They had been

Future Tense.

Sing. 1. I shall be,   Plur. 1. We shall be,
      2. Thou wilt be,   2. You will be,
      3. He will be.   3. They will be.

Future Perfect Tense.

Sing. 1. I shall have been, Plur. 1. We shall have been.
2. Thou wilt have been, 2. You will have been,
3. He will have been. 3. They will have been.

WRITE OUT TWO SENTENCES, EACH CONTAINING:

A verb in the infinitive mood, perfect tense; a verb in the indicative mood, present tense; a verb in the indicative mood, pluperfect tense; a verb in the indicative mood, future tense; a verb in the indicative mood, future perfect tense.

Potential Mood.

Present Tense.

Sing. 1. I may be, Plur. 1. We may be,
2. Thou mayst be, 2. You may be,
3. He may be. 3. They may be.

Imperfect Tense.

Sing. 1. I might be, Plur. 1. We might be,
2. Thou mightst be, 2. You might be,
3. He might be. 3. They might be.

Perfect Tense.

Sing. 1. I may have been, Plur. 1. We may have been,
2. Thou mayst have been, 2. You may have been,
3. He may have been. 3. They may have been.

Pluperfect Tense.

Sing. 1. I might have been, *Plur.* 1. We might have been,
2. Thou mightst have been, 2. You might have been,
3. He might have been. 3. They might have been.

WRITE TWO SENTENCES, EACH CONTAINING:

A verb in the potential mood, present tense; a verb in the potential mood, imperfect tense; a verb in the potential mood, perfect tense; a verb in the potential mood pluperfect tense.

Subjunctive Mood.

Present Tense.

Sing. 1. If I be, *Plur.* 1. If we be,
2. If thou be, 2. If you be,
3. If he be. 3. If they be.

Imperfect Tense.

Sing. 1. If I were, *Plur.* 1. If we were,
2. If thou wert *or* were, 2. If you were,
3. If he were. 3. If they were.

Imperative Mood.

Present Tense.

Sing. 2. Be thou *or* do thou be. *Plur.* 2. Be you *or* do you be.

VERBS.

PARTICIPLES.

Imperfect.   *Perfect.*   *Preperfect.*
being,   been,   having been

WRITE TWO SENTENCES, EACH CONTAINING:

A verb in the subjunctive mood, present tense; a verb in the subjunctive mood, imperfect tense; a verb in the imperative mood; present tense.

Conjugation of the verb LOVE.
Active Voice.
PRINCIPAL PARTS.

Present.   *Imperfect.*   *Imperfect Participle.*   *Perfect Participle*
love,   loved,   loving,   loved.

Infinitive Mood.

Present Tense.   *Perfect Tense.*
To love.   To have loved.

Indicative Mood.

Present Tense.

Sing. 1. I love,   *Plur.* 1. We love,
        2. Thou lovest,   2. You love,
        3. He loves.   3. They love.

Imperfect Tense.

Sing. 1. I loved,   *Plur.* 1. We loved,
        2. Thou lovedst,   2. You loved,
        3. He loved.   3. They loved.

Perfect Tense.

Sign: have, hast, has.

Sing. 1. I have loved, *Plur.* 1. We have loved,
2. Thou hast loved, 2. You have loved,
3. He has loved. 3. They have loved

Pluperfect Tense.

Sign: had.

Sing. 1. I had loved, *Plur.* 1. We had loved,
2. Thou hadst loved, 2. You had loved,
3. He had loved. 3. They had loved

Future Tense.

Sign: shall, will.

Sing. 1. I shall love, *Plur.* 1. We shall love,
2. Thou wilt love, 2. You will love,
3. He will love. 3. They will love.

Future Perfect Tense.

Sign: shall have, will have.

Singular. *Plural.*
1. I shall have loved, 1. We shall have loved,
2. Thou wilt have loved, 2. You will have loved,
3. He will have loved. 3. They will have loved.

WRITE TWO SENTENCES, EACH CONTAINING:

A verb in the indicative mood, present tense; a verb in the indicative mood, imperfect tense; a verb in the indicative mood, perfect tense; a verb in the indicative mood, future tense.

Potential Mood.

Present Tense.

Sign: **may, can, must.**

Sing. 1. I may love,   *Plur.* 1. We may love,
2. Thou mayst love,   2. You may love,
3. He may love.   3. They may love.

Imperfect Tense.

Sign: **might, could, would, or should.**

Sing. 1. I might love,   *Plur.* 1. We might love,
2. Thou mightst love,   2. You might love,
3. He might love.   3. They might love.

Perfect Tense.

Sign: **may, can, or must have.**

Singular.   *Plural.*
1. I may have loved,   1. We may have loved,
2. Thou mayst have loved,   2. You may have loved.
3. He may have loved.   3. They may have loved.

Pluperfect Tense.

Sign: **might, could, would, or should have.**

Singular.   *Plural.*
1. I might have loved,   1. We might have loved,
2. Thou mightst have loved,   2. You might have loved,
3. He might have loved.   3. They might have loved.

WRITE TWO SENTENCES, EACH CONTAINING:

A verb in the potential mood, present tense; a verb in the potential mood, imperfect tense; a verb in the potential mood, pluperfect tense.

Subjunctive Mood.

Present Tense.

Sing. 1. If I love, *Plur.* 1. If we love,
2. If thou love, 2. If you love,
3. If he love. 3. If they love.

Imperfect Tense.

Sing. 1. If I loved, *Plur.* 1. If we loved,
2. If thou loved, 2. If you loved,
3. If he loved. 3. If they loved.

Imperative Mood.

Present Tense.

Sing. 2. Love (thou) *or* do *Plur.* 2. Love (ye *or* you) *o*
thou love. do you love.

PARTICIPLES.

Imperfect.	*Perfect.*	*Preperfect.*
loving,	loved,	having loved.

WRITE TWO SENTENCES, EACH CONTAINING:

A verb in the subjunctive mood, present tense; a verb in the imperative mood, singular.

Progressive form of the verb STUDY.

PRINCIPAL PARTS OF THE SIMPLE VERB.

Present.	*Imperfect.*	*Imperfect Participle.*	*Perfect Participle.*
study,	studied,	studying,	studied.

VERBS.

Infinitive Mood.

Present Tense.
To be studying.

Perfect Tense.
To have been studying.

Indicative Mood.

Present Tense.

Sing. 1. I am studying,   *Plur.* 1. We are studying,
       2. Thou art studying,   2. You are studying,
       3. He is studying,   3. They are studying.

Imperfect Tense.

Sing. 1. I was studying,   *Plur.* 1. We were studying,
       2. Thou wast studying,   2. You were studying,
       3. He was studying.   3. They were studying.

Perfect Tense.

Singular.   *Plural.*
1. I have been studying,   1. We have been studying,
2. Thou hast been studying,   2. You have been studying,
3. He has been studying.   3. They have been studying.

Pluperfect Tense.

Singular.   *Plural.*
1. I had been studying,   1. We had been studying,
2. Thou hadst been studying,   2. You had been studying,
3. He had been studying.   3. They had been studying.

VERBS.

Future Tense.

Singular.
1. I shall be studying,
2. Thou wilt be studying,
3. He will be studying.

Plural.
1. We shall be studying,
2. You will be studying,
3. They will be studying.

Future Perfect Tense.

Singular.
1. I shall have been studying,
2. Thou wilt have been studying,
3. He will have been studying.

Plural.
1. We shall have been studying,
2. You will have been studying,
3. They will have been studying.

Potential Mood.

Present Tense.

Singular.
1. I may be studying,
2. Thou mayst be studying,
3. He may be studying.

Plural.
1. We may be studying,
2. You may be studying,
3. They may be studying.

Imperfect Tense.

Singular.
1. I might be studying,
2. Thou mightst be studying,
3. He might be studying.

Plural.
1. We might be studying,
2. You might be studying,
3. They might be studying.

Perfect Tense.

Singular.
1. I may have been studying,
2. Thou mayst have been studying,
3. He may have been studying.

Plural.
1. We may have been studying,
2. You may have been studying,
3. They may have been studying.

Pluperfect Tense.

Singular.
1. I might have been studying,
2. Thou mightst have been studying,
3. He might have been studying.

Plural.
1. We might have been studying,
2. You might have been studying,
3. They might have been studying.

Subjunctive Mood.

Present Tense.

Singular.
1. If I be studying,
2. If thou be studying,
3. If he be studying.

Plural.
1. If we be studying,
2. If you be studying,
3. If they be studying.

Imperfect Tense.

Singular.
1. If I were studying,
2. If thou wert *or* were studying,
3. If he were studying.

Plural.
1. If we were studying,
2. If you were studying,
3. If they were studying.

Imperative Mood.

Present Tense.

Singular. *Plural.*

2. Be (thou) studying, *or* do   2. Be ye *or* you studying, *or*
thou be studying.   do you be studying.

PARTICIPLES.

Imperfect.   *Perfect.*   *Preperfect.*
being studying,   ———   having been studying.

Conjugation of the transitive verb LOVE.
Passive Voice.

PRINCIPAL PARTS.

Present.   *Imperfect.*   *Imperfect Participle.*   *Perfect Participle*
love.   loved.   loving.   loved.

Infinitive Mood.

Present Tense.   *Perfect Tense.*
To be loved.   To have been loved.

Indicative Mood.

Present Tense.

Sing. 1. I am loved,   Plur. 1. We are loved,
      2. Thou art loved,   2. You are loved,
      3. He is loved.   3. They are loved.

Imperfect Tense.

Sing. 1. I was loved,   Plur. 1. We were loved,
      2. Thou wast loved,   2. You were loved,
      3. He was loved.   3. They were loved.

Perfect Tense.

Singular.	Plural.
1. I have been loved,	1. We have been loved,
2. Thou hast been loved,	2. You have been loved,
3. He has been loved.	3. They have been loved.

Pluperfect Tense.

Singular.	Plural.
1. I had been loved,	1. We had been loved,
2. Thou hadst been loved,	2. You had been loved,
3. He had been loved.	3. They had been loved.

Future Tense.

Singular.	Plural.
1. I shall be loved,	1. We shall be loved,
2. Thou wilt be loved,	2. You will be loved,
3. He will be loved.	3. They will be loved.

Future Perfect Tense.

Singular.	Plural.
1. I shall have been loved,	1. We shall have been loved,
2. Thou wilt have been loved,	2. You will have been loved,
3. He will have been loved.	3. They will have been loved.

Potential Mood.

Present Tense.

Singular.	Plural.
1. I may be loved,	1. We may be loved,
2. Thou mayst be loved,	2. You may be loved,
3. He may be loved.	3. They may be loved.

VERBS.

Imperfect Tense.

Singular.	*Plural.*
1. I might be loved,	1. We might be loved.
2. Thou mightst be loved,	2. You might be loved.
3. He might be loved.	3. They might be loved.

Perfect Tense.

Singular.	*Plural.*
1. I may have been loved,	1. We may have been loved,
2. Thou mayst have been loved,	2. You may have been loved.
3. He may have been loved.	3. They may have been loved.

Pluperfect Tense.

Singular.	*Plural.*
1. I might have been loved.	1. We might have been loved,
2. Thou mightst have been loved,	2. You might have been loved,
3. He might have been loved.	3. They might have been loved.

Subjunctive Mood.

Present Tense.

Singular.	*Plural.*
1. If I be loved,	1. If we be loved,
2. If thou be loved,	2. If you be loved,
3. If he be loved.	3. If they be loved.

VERBS.

Imperfect Tense.

Singular.	Plural.
1. If I were loved,	1. If we were loved,
2. If thou wert *or* were loved,	2. If you were loved,
3. If he were loved.	3. If they were loved.

Imperative Mood.

Present Tense.

Singular.
2. Be thou loved, *or* do thou be loved.

Plural.
2. Be you loved, *or* do you be loved.

PARTICIPLES.

Imperfect.	*Perfect.*	*Preperfect.*
being loved,	loved,	having been loved.

SUPPLY A SUITABLE VERB IN THE FOLLOWING:

It —— not enough to begin well, we should also —— well. God commands us to —— and —— our parents. We should —— compassion on the poor, who —— our assistance. Constant labor —— the road to success. Time —— so precious that we must not —— it. The law of God —— us not to take our neighbor's goods.

Syntax of the Verb.

1. A finite verb should agree in person and number with the nominative to which it belongs; as, John *is* good: The girls *are* studious.

VERBS.

Do not say "You was" for "You were," or "He don't know" for "He *does not* know."

2. Transitive verbs and their imperfect and preperfect participles govern the objective case; as, I saw *him* carrying *them* home.

3. The verb must be plural when its nominative is a collective noun conveying the idea of plurality. Do not say, "The jury *was* divided," for "The jury *were* divided in their opinion."

4. The verb must be singular when the nominative conveys the idea of unity. Do not say, "The army *were* defeated," instead of "The army *was* defeated."

5. When the verb has two or more nominatives, the verb must agree with them in the plural number. Do not say, "John and Albert *lives* there," instead of "*live* there."

6. When the verb has two or more singular nominatives connected by *or* or *nor*, the verb must be singular. Do not say, "Not a bat or ball *were* lost," instead of "*was* lost."

7. Do not use the imperfect tense instead of the perfect participle; as, "I should have *went* away," instead of "I should have *gone* away."

8. Do not use the *perfect participle* for the imperfect tense; as, "He *done* the work well," instead of "*did* the work well."

9. The subjunctive mood is used when we are speaking, not of a fact or of what is assumed to be a fact, but of something which is only thought of.

10. A verb in the subjunctive mood is generally preceded by *if, that, though, lest,* or *unless.*

11. When there is any doubt as to whether the indicative or subjunctive mood is required, use the indicative.

12. A verb in the infinitive mood is commonly governed

by the preposition **to**, which connects it to the other part of speech on which it depends.

13. The verbs *bid, dare, feel, let, see, make, need,* and *hear,* and sometimes *find, have, help, behold, mark, observe* and other equivalents of *see,* usually take the infinitive without the preposition **to**.

14. Intransitive verbs take the same case after as before them when both words refer to the same thing; as, *It is he; General Harrison* was elected *President.*

PARTICIPLES.

1. **A participle** is a form of the verb expressing action or state of being without limitation of person and number.

2. The participle admits of **three forms**: the imperfect, the perfect, and the preperfect.

3. The **imperfect participle** expresses action or state of being as continuing and unfinished; as, *reaping.*

4. The imperfect participle is formed by adding *ing* to the root-verb; as, *speak-ing.*

5. The **perfect participle** expresses action or state of being as past; as, *spoken.*

6. The perfect participle is formed by adding *d* or *ed* to the root of regular verbs, and *n* or *en* to the root of irregular verbs.

7. The **preperfect participle** expresses action or state of being as having been completed; as, *having spoken.*

8. The preperfect participle is formed by prefixing the word *having* to the perfect participle.

WHERE THE DASH OCCURS INSERT A SUITABLE PARTICIPLE:

The workman, —— with fatigue, fell into a deep sleep. The art of —— well and fluently is important. Henry,

—— on the pavement, and broke his leg. The retiring president —— the meeting and withdrew from the platform. Augustus has a —— for books. —— by the gale, the vessel was dashed against the rocky shore. —— his soldiers over the Alps, Hannibal entered Italy. —— with difficulties and disappointments, La Salle never lost courage. I have not —— here to-day. St. Paul, —— in the reign of Nero, was witness of his cruelty.

Syntax of the Participle.

1. Participles relate to nouns or pronouns, or they are governed by prepositions.

2. The participle should be so used that there may be no doubt as to what it modifies.

3. After verbs signifying *to omit, to avoid,* or *to prevent,* the participle, and not the infinitive, should be employed.

4. After verbs signifying *to try* or *to intend,* the infinitive, and not the participle, should be employed.

ADVERBS.

1. An **adverb** is a word used to modify a verb, an adjective, or another adverb; as, *When* you speak, speak *slowly, distinctly,* and *correctly.*

2. Adverbs are divided into **four classes**; namely, adverbs of time, of place, of degree, and of manner.

3. **Adverbs of time** answer the questions *When? How long? How soon?* or *How often?*—as, *now, then, soon, still, never, already, hereafter.*

4. **Adverbs of place** answer the questions *Where?*

ADVERBS.

Whither? Whence?—as, *here, there, yonder, where, away, above, below.*

5. Adverbs of degree answer the question *How much? How little?*—as, *more, most, fully, scarcely, chiefly.*

6. Adverbs of manner answer the question *How?*—as, *so, thus, well, ill, justly, slowly.*

7. The only modification adverbs have is **comparison**.

8. Most adverbs of manner are compared by prefixing the adverbs *more* and *most, less* and *least;* as, wisely, *more* wisely, *most* wisely; culpably, *less* culpably, *least* culpably.

MENTION THE ADVERBS ENDING IN **ly** FORMED FROM THE ADJECTIVES GIVEN:

slow—slowly,	liberal—liberally,	busy—busily,
manful ——	general ——	sole ——
pretty ——	hearty ——	whole ——
gay ——	rude ——	feeble ——

POINT OUT THE ADJECTIVES AND ADVERBS IN THE FOLLOWING SENTENCES:

The good boys spoke truthfully. The coach will start when the heavy rain ceases. The amiable girl was justly admired. The interesting book was elegantly covered. The honest soldier walked mournfully away. How dark the sky appears!

SUPPLY AN ADVERB THAT WILL COMPLETE THE SENSE:

The sincere man is —— a valuable friend. The sun had set —— the western hills. Grieve —— more. The noblest monuments —— decay. They walked so —— that their footsteps were —— heard. The room is —— hot.

Syntax of the Adverb.

1. Adverbs modify verbs, adjectives, other adverbs, and sometimes phrases or clauses.

2. Adverbs should be so placed that there be no doubt as to what words they modify.

3. Never place an adverb between "**to**" and its verb.

4. *Farther* is used with reference to distance; *further* means additional; as, I can proceed no *farther* on this road till I receive *further* instructions.

5. *Most* should not be used for *almost*.

6. *Hence, thence,* and *whence* should not be preceded by *from.*

PREPOSITIONS.

1. **A preposition** is a word used to express relation between other words.

2. A preposition is generally placed before a noun or pronoun which is called the object of the preposition.

The following are some of the principal simple prepositions:

Abroad, about, above, across, after, against, along, amid, among, around, at, before, behind, below, beneath. beyond, concerning, down, during, far, from, in, into, of, off, on, over, past, round, since, thing, till, toward, under, underneath, until, up, upon, with, within, without.

SUPPLY A SUITABLE PREPOSITION:

Struck —— a ball. Walk —— the garden. Remain —— home. Arrived —— Boston. Ride —— a car. Sent her —— school. Came —— Albany. Engrave —— marble. Raise your heart —— God. Live —— peace. He will die

CONJUNCTIONS.

—— hunger. Punish him —— stealing. Speak —— deliberation. Write —— English. It is good —— food. John differs —— him —— appearances. We sat —— a mossy bank, —— an aged pine —— whose branches the south wind made pleasant music. He acted sternly —— trifling matters. He went —— the house. His home is —— Brooklyn, and his office —— New York. The boy fell —— the water. He goes —— the house.

Syntax of the Preposition.

1. A preposition shows the relation between two terms, the latter of which it governs; as, This book is different *from* that.

2. Two prepositions are sometimes combined and used as one; as, *from among; over against; from before.*

3. The preposition *into* denotes relation produced by change from one condition or place to another; the preposition *in* expresses motion or rest, in a condition or place; hence, "to walk *into* the garden" and "to walk *in* the garden" have not the same meaning.

4. *Between* refers to **two** persons or things; among refers to **more** than **two**; as, Divide this apple *between* the *two* boys; Divide this orange *among* the *four* boys.

5. A preposition governing a pronoun is often separated from its object; as, "*Whom* did he speak *of?*"

6. Do not omit prepositions needed to complete the sense.

CONJUNCTIONS.

1. **A conjunction** is a word used to join words, phrases, or sentences; as, Matthew *and* Charles are good boys, *but* George is idle.

CONJUNCTIONS.

2. Conjunctions are divided into **two classes**: co-ordinate and subordinate.

3. A **co-ordinate conjunction** is a word that joins words, phrases, or sentences, which are of the same rank.

4. A **subordinate conjunction** is a word that joins a dependent phrase or clause with the phrase or clause on which it depends.

5. When co-ordinate or subordinate conjunctions are used in pairs and have a mutual relation they are called **correlative conjunctions**.

6. Conjunctions not only connect but they also serve to introduce a sentence ; as, *If* I were you I would remain.

The following are the principal conjunctions:

7. **Co-ordinate** : *And, as, both, because, even, for, if, that, then, since, seeing, so.*

8. **Subordinate** : *Although, or, not, neither, nor, either, except, but, yet, whether, lest, unless, save, though, notwithstanding.*

9. **Correlative** : *As—as; as—so; both—and; if—then; either—or; neither—nor; whether—or; though* or *although —yet.*

WHERE THE DASH OCCURS INSERT A SUITABLE CONJUNCTION:

Boys, keep good company —— you will be one of their number. Roll on, thou deep —— dark blue ocean. He is honest —— his judgment is poor. Time, patience —— industry overcome all obstacles. James —— Walter are studious, —— Arthur is idle.

NAME THE CONJUNCTIONS IN THE FOLLOWING SENTENCES:

Each separate death is an undisclosed secret between the

CONJUNCTIONS. 81

Creator and creature. There are good angels around us and graces are raining down upon us. Horace or Albert will go. Slowly but sadly they laid him down. He died as he had lived. James saw that she was afraid. Charles was graceful but not tall.

Syntax of the Conjunction.

1. Conjunctions connect words, phrases, or clauses.
2. When a word or phrase depends on two connected words or phrases, it should make sense with each.
3. The conjunction *than* should introduce the latter term of a comparison after *else, other, rather,* implying something different in kind, and after *all comparatives.*

Do not use conjunctions instead of other parts of speech; as, I will try *and* (instead of *to*) do better next time.

Do not use *or* as the correlative of *neither;* as, *neither* Mary *or* I, instead of *neither* Mary *nor* I. Do not use *like* instead of *as* or *as if;* as, He walked *like* (*as if*) he were lame.

Do not use *but what* for *that* or *but that;* as, I have no doubt *but what* (*that*) he did it.

Do not use *if* for *whether;* as, See *if* (*whether*) he can go.

Analysis of Compound and Complex Sentences.

1. **A compound sentence** is a sentence composed of two or more independent propositions.
2. **A complex sentence** is a sentence containing at

least two propositions, one of which is principal and the other subordinate.

3. A **clause** is a component part of a compound or complex sentence.

4. Clauses are divided into **four classes**: noun, adjective, adverbial, and explanatory.

5. A **noun clause** is one that takes the place of a noun.

6. An **adjective clause** is a clause that performs the function of an adjective.

7. An **adverbial clause** is a clause that performs the function of an adverb.

8. An **explanatory clause** is a clause that explains some noun or pronoun in a sentence.

EXAMPLES IN THE ANALYSIS OF SENTENCES.

1. *A man who employs his leisure moments well, will accomplish much during his life.*

This is a complex declarative sentence. The principal clause is *A man will accomplish much during his life;* the dependent clause is *who employs his leisure moments well;* the connective is *who.* The subject of the principal clause is *man;* the predicate is *will accomplish;* the object is *much.* The subject is limited by the article *a* and modified by the dependent clause; the predicate is modified by the simple adverbial phrase *during his life;* the object is unmodified. The principal word of the phrase is *life* which is modified by the adjective adjunct *his.* The subject of the dependent clause is *who;* the predicate *employs;* the object *moments.* The subject is unmodified; the predicate is modified by the adverb *well,* and the object by the adjective adjuncts *his* and *leisure.*

2. *Prosperity gains friends, but adversity tries them.*

This is a compound declarative sentence consisting of the two independent clauses : *Prosperity gains friends, adversity tries them;* connected by *but.* The subject of the first clause is *prosperity;* the predicate is *gains;* the object is *friends.* The subject of the second clause is *adversity;* the predicate is *tries;* the object is *them.* Neither of them has any adjuncts.

ANALYZE THE FOLLOWING SENTENCES:

The house that was sold, once belonged to my father. The books that we have, should be valued. We shall start for Philadelphia when the train arrives. Give me the money that belongs to me. Homer was the greater genius, Virgil the better artist. I will tell you the story when we meet again. That is the beautiful feather which was given to me. That it is our duty to be kind to the poor does not admit of doubt. Always remember that you owe much to your teachers. Let us then be up and doing. It was with the greatest labor that the American union was formed.

COMBINE EACH SET OF THE FOLLOWING SENTENCES INTO ONE, OMITTING ALL UNNECESSARY WORDS :

1. The tongue enables us to make known our wants.
   The tongue enables us to express our desires.

2. Labor strengthens the the body.
   Labor gives a relish for food.
   Labor is rewarded with success.

3. Politeness endears us to others.
   Politeness makes our society pleasant to others.
   Politeness is a perpetual letter of recommendation.

4. The boys broke a pane of glass.
The boys ran into the yard.
The grocer ran after them.

ANALYZE THE FOLLOWING SENTENCES:

To do good to all men is the duty of a Christian. To be disobedient towards parents is unlawful. To err is human; to forgive divine. A boy of honor will never listen to any temptation against conscience. His object was to warn his audience. My desire is to please, not to displease. To speak the truth I was to blame. Pause for awhile, O toilers of the earth, to contemplate the beauties of the universe.

SYNTAX.

Syntax treats of the relations of words in sentences.

A Summary of the Leading Rules of Syntax.

ARTICLES.

I. Articles relate to the nouns which they limit in meaning.

CASES.

II. A noun or pronoun that is the subject of a finite verb is put in the nominative case.

III. A noun or pronoun in the possessive case is governed by another noun with which the former generally stands in the relation of possession.

IV. A noun or pronoun, the object of an action or of a relation, is put in the objective case.

V. Intransitive verbs take the same case after as before them when both words mean the same person or thing.

VI. A noun or pronoun used to explain a noun or pronoun going before is in the same case.

VII. A noun or pronoun not depending upon its connection with any other word in the sentence, is put in the nominative case absolute.

Pronouns.

VIII. A pronoun must agree with its antecedent in gender, number, and person.

Adjectives.

IX. Adjectives relate to the nouns or pronouns that they qualify or describe.

Verbs.

X. A finite verb must agree with its subject or nominative in person and number.

XI. The preposition **to** governs the infinitive mood, and connects it with some preceding word.

XII. When a **conditional clause** expresses a hope, a wish, or a thought containing the **idea of futurity**, the verb should be in the **subjunctive mood**.

Participles.

XIII. Participles relate to nouns or pronouns, or else are governed by prepositions.

PREPOSITIONS.

XIV. A preposition expresses the relation between the noun or pronoun following it and some other word, or words, in a sentence.

CONJUNCTIONS.

XV. Conjunctions connect words or clauses.

INTERJECTIONS.

XVI. The interjection has no grammatical relation to the other parts of a sentence.

EXERCISES IN SYNTAX.

Analysis and Parsing.

SIMPLE SENTENCES.

I. *The boy studied his lessons.*

This is a simple declarative sentence. The subject is *boy;* the predicate is *studied;* and the object is *lessons;* adjunct of subject, *the;* adjunct of object, *his.*

The is the definite article, and relates to the noun *boy,* according to the rule: Articles relate to the nouns which they limit in meaning.

Boy is a common noun, third person, singular number, masculine gender, and nominative case, according to the rule: A noun that is the subject of a finite verb must be in the nominative case.

Studied is a regular transitive verb, active voice, indicative mood, imperfect tense, and agrees with the noun *boy* in person and number, according to the rule.

His is a personal pronoun, third person, singular number, masculine gender, and possessive case, according to the rule: A noun or pronoun in the possessive case is governed by another noun with which the former generally stands in the relation of possession.

Lessons is a common noun, third person, plural number, neuter gender, and objective case, according to the rule: A noun or pronoun, the object of an action or of a relation, is put in the objective case.

II. *Spare moments are the gold-dust of time.*

This is a simple declarative sentence. The subject is *moments*; the predicate is *are*; the attribute is *gold-dust*; the adjunct of the subject is *spare*; the predicate has no adjunct; the adjuncts of the attribute are *the* and the phrase *of time*.

Spare is a common adjective of the positive degree, and relates to the noun *moments*, according to the rule: Adjectives relate to the nouns or pronouns which they qualify or describe.

Moments is a common noun, third person, plural number, neuter gender, and nominative case, according to the rule: A noun or pronoun which is the subject of a finite verb must be in the nominative case.

Are is an irregular intransitive verb, indicative mood, present tense, and agrees with *moments* in person and number, according to the rule: A finite verb must agree in person and number with its subject or nominative.

The is the definite article, and relates to the noun *gold-dust*, according to the rule: Articles relate to the nouns which they limit in meaning.

Gold-dust is a common noun, third person, singular number, neuter gender, and in the nominative case after *are*, according to the rule: Intransitive verbs take the same case after as before them when both words mean the same person or thing.

Of is a preposition, and shows the relation between *gold-dust* and *time*, according to the rule: A preposition expresses the relation between the noun or pronoun following it and some other word, or words, in a sentence.

Time is a common noun, third person, singular number, neuter gender, and objective case, according to the rule: A noun which is the object of an action or a relation is put in the objective case.

III. *Life is an isthmus between two eternities.*

This is a simple declarative sentence. The subject is *life;* the predicate is *is ;* and the attribute is *isthmus;* the adjuncts of the attribute are *an* and the phrase *between two eternities.*

Life is a common noun, third person, singular number, neuter gender, and nominative case, according to the rule: A noun or pronoun that is the subject of a finite verb is put in the nominative case.

Is is an irregular intransitive verb, indicative mood, present tense, and agrees with its subject in person and number, according to the rule: A finite verb must agree with its subject or nominative in person and number.

An is the indefinite article, and relates to the noun *isthmus*, according to the rule: Articles relate to the nouns of which they limit the meaning.

Isthmus is a common noun, third person, singular number, neuter gender, and in the nominative case, according to the rule: Intransitive verbs take the same case after as before them when both words mean the same person or thing.

Between is a preposition, and shows the relation between *isthmus* and *eternities*, according to the rule: A preposition expresses the relation between the noun or pronoun following it and some other word, or words, in the same sentence.

Two is a numeral adjective, and relates to the noun *eternities*, according to the rule: Adjectives relate to the nouns or pronouns that they qualify or describe.

Eternities is a common noun, third person, singular number, neuter gender, and objective case, according to the rule: A noun or pronoun that is used as the object of an action or a relation is put in the objective case.

IV. *He who studies, acquires knowledge.*

This is a complex declarative sentence. The principal clause is *he acquires knowledge;* and the dependent clause is *who studies;* the connective word is *who.* The subject of the principal clause is *he;* the predicate is *acquires,* and the object, *knowledge;* the adjunct of the subject is the relative clause *who studies.* The subject of the dependent clause is *who;* the predicate is *studies.*

He is a personal pronoun, third person, singular number, masculine gender, and nominative case, according to the rule: A noun or pronoun that is the subject of a finite verb must be in the nominative case.

Who is a relative pronoun, and agrees with its antecedent *he* in gender, number, and person, according to the rule: A pronoun must agree with its antecedent in gender, number, and person.

Studies is a regular transitive verb, active voice, indicative mood, present tense, and agrees with *who* in person and number, according to the rule: A finite verb must agree with its subject or nominative in person and number.

Acquires is a regular transitive verb, active voice, indicative mood, present tense, and agrees with *he* in person and number, according to the rule: A finite verb must agree with its subject or nominative in person and number.

Knowledge is a common noun, third person, singular number, neuter gender, and objective case, according to the rule: A noun or pronoun that is the object of an action or a relation is put in the objective case.

V. *Science may bring you honor, but virtue alone can make you happy.*

This is a compound declarative sentence. The first member is *science may bring you honor;* the second is *only virtue can make you happy;* the connective word is *but.* The subject of the first member is *science;* the predicate is *may bring;* the object is *honor;* the adjunct of the predicate is the phrase (*to*) *you.* The subject of the second member is *virtue;* the predicate is *can make;* the object is *you;* the adjunct of the subject is *only*, and the adjunct of the object is *happy.*

Science is a common noun, third person, singular number, neuter gender, and nominative case, according to the rule: A noun or pronoun that is the subject of a finite verb must be in the nominative case.

May bring is an irregular transitive verb, active voice, potential mood, present tense, and agrees with *science* in person and number, according to the rule: A finite verb must agree with its subject or nominative in person and number.

You is a personal pronoun, second person, plural number, masculine gender, and objective case, according to the rule: A noun or pronoun that is the object of an action or a relation is put in the objective case.

Honor is a common noun, third person, singular number, neuter gender, and objective case, according to the rule: A noun or pronoun that is the object of an action or a relation is put in the objective case.

SYNTAX.

But is a conjunction, and connects the two clauses of the compound sentence, according to the rule: Conjunctions connect words or clauses.

Alone is a pronominal adjective, and relates to the noun *virtue*, according to the rule: Adjectives relate to the nouns or pronouns which they qualify or describe.

Virtue is a common noun, third person, singular number, neuter gender, and nominative case, according to the rule: A noun or pronoun that is the subject of a finite verb is put in the nominative case.

Can make is an irregular transitive verb, active voice, potential mood, present tense, and agrees with *virtue* in person and number, according to the rule: A finite verb must agree with its subject or nominative in person and number.

You is a personal pronoun, second person, plural number, masculine gender, and objective case, according to the rule: A noun or pronoun the object of an action or a relation is put in the objective case.

Happy is a common adjective, and relates to the pronoun *you*, according to the rule: Adjectives relate to the nouns or pronouns which they qualify or describe.

EXERCISES.

Under the Article.

GIVE THE SYNTAX OF THE ITALICIZED WORDS IN THE FOLLOWING:

The story was not believed.   I have a box.
> *The* way was long, *the* wind was cold,
> *The* minstrel was infirm and old;
> His withered cheek and tresses gray
> Seemed to have known *a* better day.

Correct the following:

1. William is a honorable person.
2. It is not a happiness to live with such an one.
3. The general was another sort of a man.
4. Mary is a better musician than a reader.

Under the Cases.

Give the syntax of the italicized words in the following:

Read with a *purpose*. Lay out for *yourself* a definite *object*, and let all *your reading* converge upon that *object* until *your purpose* is attained. *This* is the only *reading that* will be remembered.

On a bright *night*, twenty *minutes* rarely pass at any *part* of the *earth's surface* without the *appearance* of at least one *meteor*.

> *They* led a *lion* from *his den*,
> The *lord* of *Afric's* sun-scorched *plain;*
> And there *he* stood, stern *foe* of *men*,
> And shook *his* flowing *mane*.

Why are the following sentences incorrect?

1. Are they not wolves in sheeps' clothing?
2. Is it him, that is there?
3. This is between you and I.
4. Me and Peter generally go to school together.
5. Them is the things we need.
6. This letter is from Richard, he that is in Europe.

SYNTAX.

Under the Adjective.

GIVE THE SYNTAX OF THE ITALICIZED WORDS IN THE FOLLOWING:

If *people* are to live happily together, *they* must not fancy, because *they* are thrown together now, that *all their lives* have been exactly *similar* up to the *present time*, that *they* started exactly alike, and that they are to be for the future of the *same* mind.

He wore *few ornaments*, and usually the *same;* but *these* were of *great* price. His *manners, frank* and *soldierlike*, concealed a most *cool* and *calculating* spirit.

CORRECT THE FOLLOWING SENTENCES:

1. William and James arrived safely.
2. In English two negatives destroy one another.
3. Do not take the latter of these three.
4. Eve was the fairest of all her daughters.
5. He seems the most wisest.

Under the Pronoun.

GIVE THE SYNTAX OF THE ITALICIZED WORDS IN THE FOLLOWING:

This is *the man that* committed the *deed*. The *horse* which *Alexander* rode was called *Bucephalus*. *That* was the *work* of Herod, *which* is but *another* name for cruelty. Keep at *your* book or your *subject-matter* till *you* have finished *it*.

CORRECT THE FOLLOWING SENTENCES:

1. Is that the man which I saw?
2. Them is the dogs which swam the river.
3. Every one should mind their own business.
4. John is the person what I want to see.
5. There is no more oats. The horse has eaten all of it.

Under the Verb.

GIVE THE SYNTAX OF THE ARTICLES, NOUNS, PRONOUNS, ADJECTIVES, AND VERBS IN THE FOLLOWING:

A great elm-tree spread its broad branches over it, at the foot of which bubbled up a spring of the softest and sweetest water, in a little well formed of a barrel, and then stole sparkling away through the grass, to a neighboring brook, that babbled along among alders and dwarf willows.

> Brightest and best of the sons of the morning,
> Dawn on our darkness, and lend us thine aid.
> Star of the East, the horizon adorning,
> Guide where our infant Redeemer is laid.

CORRECT THE FOLLOWING SENTENCES:

1. You was disappointed.
2. Them things comes from Europe.
3. Mary dares not to speak of John's absence.
4. No book or paper are in this desk.
5. Neither of them boys have any sense.
6. I aint got nothing.
7. He don't know nothing.
8. I seen him yesterday.
9. He said, " Who is you ?"
10. I have seen him last week.

Under the Adverb.

GIVE THE SYNTAX OF THE ADVERBS IN THE FOLLOWING SENTENCES:

This is where my brother works. The place whither you are travelling is far away from Russia. The oak is still lying where it fell. Henrietta is going to the park; Mabel is going also. The moon rose after the sun had set. We shall hear ere noon.

> Down in a green and shady bed
> A modest violet grew.

CORRECT THE FOLLOWING SENTENCES:

1. That boy writes good.
2. He spoke sharp to his servant.
3. You need not to speak no more.
4. From whence is this man?
5. He is not as good as you imagine.

Under the Preposition and the Conjunction.

GIVE THE SYNTAX OF THE PREPOSITIONS AND CONJUNCTIONS IN THE FOLLOWING:

> A barge across Loch Katrine flew,
> High stood the henchman on the prow.

The mild southern breeze brought a shower from the hill. The soldier arrived while we were speaking of him. Go with him.

CORRECT THE FOLLOWING:

1. It was no other but my own friend.
2. I do not deny but they have merit.
3. Neither write or speak of this affair.
4. He does not think this is so good as that.

PUNCTUATION.

Punctuation is the art of dividing a sentence into its component parts by certain marks, or points.

The principal marks of punctuation are:

The period (.)	The exclamation (!)
The colon (:)	The dash (—)
The semicolon (;)	The parenthesis ( )
The comma (,)	The brackets [ ]
The interrogation (?)	The quotation points (" ").

I.—*The Period.*

1. The **period** is placed at the end of every complete, declarative, or imperative sentence; as, *A continual dropping wears the stone. Never lose a moment of time.*

2. The **period** is employed to mark abbreviations; as, A.D., for Anno Domini; M.D., for Medical Doctor.

II.—*The Colon.*

1. The **colon** is placed between the greater divisions of a sentence, when minor subdivisions are separated by semicolons; as, "We perceive the shadow to have moved along the dial, but did not see it moving; we observe that the grass has grown, though it was impossible to see it grow: so the advances we make in knowledge, consisting of minute and gradual steps, are perceivable only after intervals of time."

2. The **colon** is employed to introduce a general statement, or a direct quotation when referred to by the words *thus, following, as follows, this, these,* and the like; as, "Three elements enter into history: person, place, and time." "Remember the golden rule: 'Do unto others as you would have others do unto you.'" "He answered my argument thus: 'The man who lives by hope, will die by despair.'"

III.—*The Semicolon.*

1. The **semicolon** is placed between the members of compound sentences, not very closely connected; as, "Brutes are governed by instinct; man, by his reason."

2. The **semicolon** is placed between the greater divisions of a sentence, when minor divisions occur separated by the **comma**; as, "The poisoned valley of Java is twenty miles in extent, and of considerable width; it presents a most desolate appearance, being entirely destitute of vegetation."

3. The **semicolon** is placed before the words *as, namely, viz., that is,* when they introduce an example or a specification of particulars. For an illustration, see the preceding Rule.

IV.—*The Comma.*

1. The **comma** is used to separate the similar parts of a proposition; as, "Learn patience, calmness, self-command, and disinterestedness."

2. When words are joined *in pairs* by conjunctions, the pairs should be separated by the **comma**; as, "Old and young, rich and poor, wise and foolish, were involved."

3. A **parenthetical** clause, phrase, or word, must be separated from the rest of the sentence by the **comma**; as, "Man, *created in the image of God*, has an immortal soul."

4. The **comma** is usually inserted in place of a finite verb that is understood; as, "To err is human; to forgive, divine."

5. The name of a person or thing addressed, or the part of a sentence transposed, is separated from the rest of the sentence by the **comma**; as, "John, respect the aged." "*Of all our senses,* sight is the most important."

6. The **comma** is generally used between the simple

members of compound sentences, when they are very short; as, "Love not sleep, lest thou come to poverty."

7. **A short quotation,** or one introduced by the verbs *say, reply, cry,* is generally separated from the rest of the sentence by the **comma**; as, "'I shall arrive in Paris to-morrow morning,' replied the traveller." "Captain Lawrence cried out, 'Do not give up the ship.'" "There is much in the proverb, *No pains, no gains.*"

8. The **comma** is used before *or* introducing an equivalent, or a clause explaining the writer's meaning; as, "Spelter, or zinc, comes chiefly from Germany."

9. The **comma** is used to separate words or clauses denoting comparison, or contrast; as, "Return a kindness, not an injury." "He gave me an apple, not an orange." "As three is to six, so is four to eight."

V.—*The Interrogation.*

1. The **point of interrogation** is used after every interrogative sentence, clause, or word; as, "Do not the heavens proclaim the glory of God?"

VI.—*The Exclamation.*

1. The **exclamation** is placed after every exclamatory sentence, clause, or word; as, "How it snows!" "The clock is striking midnight; how solemn the sound!" "Unfortunate man that he is, what has he done!" Alas! Poor Yorick.

VII.—*The Dash.*

1. The **dash** is used to mark a sudden interruption or transition; as, "He is always right—in his own opinion."

2. The **dash** is also used (1) to set off a parenthetical

expression, (2) before a repetition made for effect, or with a view to further explanation, (3) to mark an omission, or (4) a more considerable pause than the structure of the sentence would seem to require; as, "The enemy fled—they had fought us all day—none too soon to save their shattered forces." "Ours is a glorious country—a country blessed above all others." "In the year 18—, a terrible calamity befell that city." "Now they part—to meet no more."

VIII.—*The Parenthesis.*

1. The **parenthesis** is used to enclose a remark, a quotation, or a date, that may be omitted without breaking the construction or injuring the sense of the sentence; as, "This doctrine (so John would have us believe) is false."

IX.—*The Brackets.*

1. The **brackets** are used to enclose what one person puts into the writings of another, as a correction, an explanation, or an omission; as, "He [the orator] stated the fact differently."

X.—*The Quotation Points.*

1. The **quotation points** are used to distinguish words that are repeated literally from their author; as, He tells us, "Do not attempt to read all [magazine articles]."

2. A quotation within a passage which is itself quoted, is set off by **single points** (' '); as, It has been well said, "The command, 'Thou shalt not kill,' forbids many crimes besides murder."

LETTER WRITING.

1. **A Letter** is a prose composition addressed to some person or persons.

2. **Private Letters** are those intended for the persons only to whom they are addressed.

3. **Public Letters** are essays or reports, in letter form, intended for the public.

Form of a Letter.

Custom has sanctioned certain forms for LETTERS. The parts of a Letter are the *heading*, the *introduction*, the *body*, the *conclusion*, and the *superscription*.

The **heading** consists of the place from which the Letter is sent and the date of writing; as,

Boston, June 5, 1890.

or

243 *Park Ave.,*
New York, April 29, 1875.

The **introduction** contains the name and post-office address of the person to whom the letter is written, and the salutation; as,

Mr. George Brown,
Brooklyn, N. Y.,
Dear Sir.

Letters to friends are begun in a less formal manner. Where persons are intimate they generally address each other by the Christian name; as,

My dear George; My dear Mary.

A form of address frequently used is this:

Dear Mr. Gilman; Dear Mrs. Kernan.

LETTER WRITING.

- The **body** of the Letter contains what the writer wishes to say to the person to whom it is written, and it contains as many paragraphs as there are distinct topics.

The **conclusion** contains a complimentary close and the name of the person sending the Letter; as, *Yours truly, Respectfully yours, Very respectfully yours, Faithfully yours, Sincerely yours,* etc.

The **superscription** is the name and post-office address of the person to whom the Letter is written.

                            (Heading.)
                        48 Bedford St.,
                      New York, May 12, 1890.

(The Address.)
My dear Parents:

                  (Body.)
   *It*_____

_____

_____

_____

   *You*_____

_____

_____

_____

                    (Conclusion.)
          Ever affectionately yours,
                    H—— C——.

(Superscription.)

Mr. Charles Steward,
124 West Street,
New York City.

Stamp

APPENDIX.

LISTS OF IRREGULAR VERBS.

I. *Verbs that Vary in all Three Parts.*

Present.	Imperfect.	Perfect Participle.
am or be	was	been
arise	arose	arisen
bear (*to bring forth*)	bore, **bare**	born
bear (*to uphold*)	bore, **bare**	borne
beat	beat, bet	**beaten**, or beat
begin	began	begun
bid	bid, **bade**	**bidden**, bid
bite	bit	**bitten**, bit
blow	blew	blown
break	broke, **brake**	broken
chide	chid	**chidden**, chid
choose	chose	chosen
cleave (*to split*)	**clove**, cleft	**cloven**, cleft
come	came	come
do	did	done
draw	drew	drawn
drink	drank	drank, **drunk**
drive	drove	driven
eat	**ate**, eat	**eaten**, or eat
fall	fell	fallen
fly	flew	flown
forbear	forbore	forborne

108

APPENDIX.

Present.	*Imperfect.*	*Perfect Participle.*
forget	forgot	forgotten, forgot
forsake	forsook	forsaken
freeze	froze	frozen
get	got	gotten, got
give	gave	given
go	went	gone
grow	grew	grown
hide	hid	hidden, hid
hold	held	held, holden
know	knew	known
lade (*to load*)	laded	laden
lie (*to recline*)	lay	lain
ride	rode	ridden
ring	rang, rung	rung
rise	rose	risen
run	ran, run	run
see	saw	seen
shake	shook	shaken
shrink	shrank	shrunk
sing	sang, sung	sung
sink	sank, sunk	sunk
slay	slew	slain
smite	smote	smitten, smit
speak	spoke, spake	spoken
spit	spit, spat	spit, spitten, spitted
spring	sprang, sprung	sprung
steal	stole	stolen
stride	strode	stridden
strive	strove	striven
swear	swore	sworn
swim	swam, swum	swum
take	took	taken
tear	tore	torn
throw	threw	thrown
tread	trod	trodden, trod
wear	wore, ware	worn
write	wrote	written, writ
weave	wove	woven, wove

APPENDIX.

2. Verbs whose Imperfect Tense and Perfect Participles are Alike.

Present.	Imperfect.	Perfect Participle.
abide	abode	abode
bend	bent	bent
beseech	besought	besought
bet	bet	bet
bind	bound	bound
bleed	bled	bled
breed	bred	bred
bring	brought	brought
burst	burst	burst
buy	bought	bought
cast	cast	cast
catch	caught	caught
cling	clung	clung
cost	cost	cost
creep	crept	crept
cut	cut	cut
dig	dug	dug
feed	fed	fed
feel	felt	felt
fight	fought	fought
find	found	found
flee	fled	fled
fling	flung	flung
grind	ground	ground
have	had	had
hear	heard	heard
hit	hit	hit
hurt	hurt	hurt
keep	kept	kept
lay	laid	laid
lead	led	led
leave	left	left
lend	lent	lent
let	let	let
lose	lost	lost

Present.	Imperfect.	Perfect Participle.
make	made	made
mean	meant	meant
meet	met	met
pay	paid	paid
put	put	put
read	read	read
rend	rent	rent
rid	rid	rid
say	said	said
seek	sought	sought
sell	sold	sold
send	sent	sent
set	set	set
shed	shed	shed
shine	shone	shone
shoe	shod	shod
shoot	shot	shot
shut	shut	shut
sit	sat	sat
sleep	slept	slept
slide	slid	slid
sling	slung	slung
slink	slunk	slunk
slit	slit	slit, slitted
speed	sped	sped
spend	spent	spent
spin	spun	spun
split	split	split
spread	spread	spread
stand	stood	stood
stick	stuck	stuck
sting	stung	stung
strike	struck	struck
string	strung	strung
sweep	swept	swept
swing	swung	swung
teach	taught	taught
tell	told	told
think	thought	thought

APPENDIX. 107

Present.	Imperfect.	Perfect Participle.
thrust	thrust	thrust
weep	wept	wept
win	won	won
wind	wound	wound
wring	wrung	wrung

3. Verbs both Regular and Irregular in their Principal Parts.

Present.	Imperfect.	Perfect Participle.
awake	awoke, awaked	awaked
bereave	bereft, bereaved	bereft, bereaved
blend	blended	blended, blent
build	built, builded	built, builded
burn	burned, burnt	burned, burnt
cleave (*to cling to*)	cleaved, clave	cleaved
climb	climbed, clomb	climbed
clothe	clothed, clad	clothed, clad
crow	crowed, crew	crowed
dare (*to venture*)	dared, durst	dared
deal	dealt, dealed	dealt, dealed
dream	dreamed, dreamt	dreamed, dreamt
dwell	dwelt, dwelled	dwelt, dwelled
gild	gilded, gilt	gilded, gilt
gird	girded, girt	girded, girt
grave	graved	graven, graved
hang	hung, hanged	hung, hanged
hew	hewed	hewn, hewed
kneel	knelt, kneeled	knelt, kneeled
knit	knit, knitted	knit, knitted
light	lighted, lit	lighted, lit
mow	mowed	mown, mowed
pen (*to inclose*)	pent, penned	pent, penned
quit	quit, quitted	quit, quitted
rive	rived	riven, rived
rot	rotted	rotten, rotted

Present.	Imperfect.	Perfect Participle.
saw	sawed	sawn, sawed
shape	shaped	shapen, shaped
shave	shaved	shaven, shaved
shear	sheared	shorn, sheared
show	showed	shown, showed
sow	sowed	sown, sowed
spell	spelt, spelled	spelt, spelled
spill	spilt, spilled	spilt, spilled
strew	strewed	strewn, strewed
strow	strowed	strown, strowed
swell	swelled	swollen, swelled
thrive	thrived, throve	thriven, thrived
wax	waxed	waxen, waxed
whet	whet, whetted	whet, whetted
work	wrought, worked	wrought, worked

DEFECTIVE VERBS.

The Following List Contains all the Defective Verbs.

Present.	Imperfect.	Present.	Imperfect.
beware	——	shall	should
can	could	will	would
may	might	quoth	quoth
methinks	methought	wis	wist
must	must	wit	wot
ought	ought		

THE END.